My Rights
are *Divine*

A Closer Look at Children's Rights
in the Muslim Arab World

Nina Abdul Razzak

authorHOUSE®

AuthorHouse™ UK Ltd.
1663 Liberty Drive
Bloomington, IN 47403 USA
www.authorhouse.co.uk
Phone: 0800.197.4150

Published by AuthorHouse 09/16/2014

ISBN: 978-1-4969-9135-5 (sc)
ISBN: 978-1-4969-9136-2 (e)

This book is dedicated to all children
who have endured some kind of violation of their human rights,
to let them know that their voices must be heard.

Contents

Preface

This book came about because of my desire to demonstrate that that there is still hope for child abuse victims in the Muslim Arab World, due to there being individuals willing to stand up for their rights and to speak in their name. More importantly, though, my aspiration through this work was to eventually prove that the hope for child victims becomes greater in the presence of a special type of culture- one that truly understands that no child should be left to suffer in silence and in which children are given the chance to loudly sound their voice in issues concerning their rights as humans. This work makes the argument that a culture in which *true* or *authentic* Islamic values are rightly implemented measures up to being such a culture. To be able to put forth such an argument, I first had to see, describe, and tell things and facts as they are, regardless of their ruthlessness in some cases. In other words, I had to tread the path of constructive criticism, in order to draw a clear roadmap that could possibly result in some positive social change in the region.

Although this book's scope focuses on the Muslim Arab World, it can be of interest and benefit to readers from other cultures and religious backgrounds. The reason for this is that this book manages to combine Arabic and Islamic perspectives and realities, on the one hand, with Western theories, models, and scientific research data on the other. There is therefore so much to be learnt from this combination, regardless of one's affiliation and geographical location, and there is a lot of benefit to be gained from the arguments, analyses, and recommendations made in this book in general. In particular, social contexts similar to the Muslim Arab World in their socioeconomic development level, cultural peculiarities, and common problems, can be impacted greatly by the contents of this work. The fact that the book's approach is interdisciplinary in nature, also adds to its value and makes it available to a wider audience. In specific, readers will get a chance to be exposed to and to educate themselves about:

- ❖ Children's rights in Islam and their status in the Muslim Arab World;
- ❖ The region's position towards international children's rights conventions;
- ❖ Types of violations of children's rights and abuse existing in the region;
- ❖ Possible explanations of why such violations exist;
- ❖ Causes and effects of child abuse and neglect in general;
- ❖ Child custody and the prevalence in the Arab World of a neglected area of emotional abuse known as parental alienation;
- ❖ The relationship between mental illness and child abuse;
- ❖ Actual cases of child maltreatment extracted from news reports from the region; and finally,
- ❖ How child protection and prevention of abuse could be practically ensured to a higher degree in the Muslim Arab World and what crucial role could be played by education in the process.

Writing this book proved to be no easy task, especially due to (1) the scarcity of resources and statistics pertaining to violation of children's rights and abuse in the Arab World; (2) the multifaceted nature and sensitivity of the topic; and (3) the emotional arousal a topic such as this is capable of producing in any human being tackling it as an issue. Despite all this, the book had to be written, simply because our children are worth it and deserve better...

By focusing here on Islam and the predominantly Muslim cultures in the Arab World, I in no way intentionally mean to ignore or depreciate the value of other religions or ethnicities existing in the Arab region. The reason behind my focus is simply the fact that the constitutions of most Arab countries are based on Islam and, demographically, their populations are mainly Muslim. Besides, tackling social problems in the Muslim communities is the area where my primary interests and curiosity lie.

Naturally, plenty of references are made in this book to the holy Quran and all the Quranic verses referred to in it are based on a translated version by Abdullah Yusuf Ali, published in 2009 by *The Other Press*. It is important to note that the holy Quran is made up of a number of chapters (known in Arabic as *souwar)* and each chapter consists of a specific number of verses (*ayat).* Each chapter has a specific title and all the chapters are numbered based on their order in the Quran. The verses are also numbered based on their order of appearance within the particular chapter they comprise. References in this book to specific chapters and verses of the holy Quran are, therefore, sometimes made by their numbers and in several cases, titles of chapters and even whole verses are actually mentioned based on the context. There is also some reference to the sayings and deeds (or *Hadith* as they are called in Arabic) of the Prophet Muhammad (*Peace be upon him).* Since the aim of this work is neither to provide a detailed examination or analysis of the Quran or the *Hadith* nor to present different interpretations of them, little is mentioned about the multiple Islamic juristic schools and their diverse perspectives and explanations. I in no way claim to be an expert in Islamic studies and, therefore, have preferred to rely- in the arguments made in this book- primarily on general and common understandings of certain Islamic concepts and principles. I have preferred this over delving into unfamiliar and complex grounds created sometimes by the divergent viewpoints coming from the multiple Islamic juristic schools. Besides, one of my main goals through this work has been from the start to present an account of things that is not simply theoretical and analytic but rather something more practical and applicable. Employing common understandings of certain Islamic concepts and principles, to tackle a serious social issue existing in the Muslim Arab World, seems to me to be of higher priority and real-world relevance than theorizing about the discrepancies of the multiple juristic schools.

Introduction

I was sitting in a plane, completely engrossed in Azar Nafisi's masterpiece *Reading Lolita In Tehran,* when the idea penetrated my mind like lightening penetrates the sky on a wild and stormy night. The idea was not totally new to me. The thought of writing a book about a topic that has been occupying my mind for several years now, had crossed my thoughts many a time before. The only difference is that on this visit, the idea did not come stripped and bare like it always did on previous occasions. Rather, it came wrapped in a strikingly appealing gown that for an instant stole both my breath and my mind. This gown of magnificence, which gracefully swathed my thought of writing this book, consisted of a million colors. Those colors were to become the points of focus of my work at a later stage.

Azar Nafisi's words seem to have that magical effect on her readers, by which she can effortlessly stimulate in their minds an array of thoughts with almost every point she makes. Her words at that time had definitely captivated me and acted like the fuel my mind needed to start its fire. Nafisi's analytic approach and constructive criticism of the problems in her own social context, in particular, were a great inspiration to me, due to the impact they've had on me as a reader- in brief, an impact of making me want to adopt the same critical approach towards my own social context, out of pure desire to hopefully bring about some kind of positive social change.

Since it is impossible to tackle all types of problems in one's social context, I've chosen to focus only on the topic that has been haunting me for years now, not only because it is one of personal interest to me but also because it affects people from all over the world and is an issue that is always coupled with pain and torment to humanity. It is the issue of child abuse and failure to protect children's inalienable rights to safety and security. After a period of thorough and meticulous research, I have come to realize that no country in the world is immune of this problem and that even the most developed societies have not yet been able to create infallible and complete systems to deal with such cases. Imagine, thus, what the situation is like in the underdeveloped and developing countries with their corresponding social contexts.

This work, therefore, addresses the issue of child abuse in the Muslim Arab World context in specific. The Arab World, better known as the *Arab Nation* or in Arabic *Al-ummah Al-arabiyah*, consists of twenty-two countries, which are: Algeria, Bahrain, Comoros, Djibouti, Egypt, Iraq, Jordan, Kuwait, Lebanon, Libya, Mauritania, Morocco, Oman, Palestine, Qatar, Saudi Arabia, Somalia, Sudan, Syria, Tunisia, United Arab Emirates, and Yemen. Although, these countries encompass groups of non-Arab origins (e.g. Kurds and Berbers) and although they are home for a number of religious faiths, the focus here, in particular, is on the Muslim Arab populations existing in the region and on the phenomenon of child abuse in it. The issue of abuse is attended to from an interdisciplinary perspective combining the fields of philosophy, religion, psychology, and education while simultaneously relying in many instances on statistical data and reviews of research findings. This, as a result, explains both the descriptive as well as the normative nature of the work's ideas and arguments; for, its main purpose is not to simply report on a particular issue or state of affairs but rather to also raise awareness of what needs to be done to tackle this issue on both the individual as well as the community level.

My genuine desire is for this book to succeed in demonstrating how child abuse could be curbed in the Muslim Arab World, since preventive measures are really in our hands. They are actually a part of a binding force that impacts almost each and every step we take in life; that force is simply *Islam-* our religion, which does not only define our relationship with God (*Allah*) Almighty but is also in actuality a way of life. This work makes the argument that a culture in which *true* or *authentic* Islamic values are rightly implemented measures up to being one that safeguards and recognizes the rights granted to children by no one other than their merciful and gracious creator *Allah*.

Chapter One

Admitting Our Faults:
A Pinch of Philosophy

Need for Facing the Facts

As was included in the 1989 Arab Organization for Human Rights (AOHR) report, the Arab World at the country level, has plenty of institutions concerned with human rights issues in general. These institutions include press and bar associations, trade union organizations, and associations of writers and publishers. When things come down to the rights of children and their protection from abuse, however, the Arab World has only recently started taking somewhat serious strides in that direction and in most of its countries, what is being done is still lacking and deficient. Probably one of the main reasons for this is that the concept of children's rights, in general, falls under the concept of human rights and although there exists in the Arab World a genuine human rights movement, it has not yet succeeded in achieving considerable significant gains (Chase & Hamzawy, 2006). For one of the challenges facing Arab human rights groups has to do with the cultural perception of the concept of 'human rights' as being a foreign concept. This results in lack of support and legitimacy in the region for the activism of these groups (Chase & Hamzawy, 2006). While this may be a contributing factor to the problem of child abuse and lack of sufficient protection of children's rights, it is not the whole story. It sometimes seems that our Arab World's long-lived pride in strong family ties has blinded it to see and accept that we too have, in our societies,

1

violations of children's rights and that our homes are not all the colorful and safe havens our pride pictures them to be. What adds to our blindness is that, in many of our cultures, religion is used (or to speak more accurately *abused*) as the shades behind which we hide to protect ourselves from the harsh realities around us. If one were to speak in Freudian terms, religion in our case seems to act as one of the best defense mechanisms by which our societies protect their egos. For, it is quite simple for any society to assume that since its individuals were born into a certain religion and since they all *appear* to be adhering to that religion's principles, then such atrocious violations like child abuse are nonexistent or at least not so grave.

Failing to Adopt True Islamic Values

Religion, in particular Islam, is in its essence capable of instilling in us values that would help us focus not only on avoiding infringements of rights but more so on dealing with one another in the most merciful of ways. The truth however is that being born in a Muslim society does not necessarily guarantee that one develops and- more importantly- acts according to such values. In brief, our societies, like other societies in the world, are far from perfect and are actually full of ills, breaches, and violations. This is not because there is something wrong with the religion itself but rather due to the lack of proper implementation of its true teachings.

We have to stress here the concept of "true teachings", since there is considerable variation in the origins, cultures, and distribution of Muslims across the globe and "what is 'Islamic' in one context has no Islamic relevance in another and much of what is non- or even un-Islamic is paraded under that banner" (Mahmood, 2004; 5). Focusing on "true teachings", therefore, helps us avoid the pitfall of making simplistic generalizations and holistic explanations that lack credibility. What are the true teachings of Islam however? They basically consist of the Quranic teachings and (*Peace be upon him*) Prophet Muhammad's sayings and deeds (or *Hadith* as they are called in Arabic). True teachings are the essence of Islam and this essence unfortunately often gets overshadowed by the so-called mere Islamic trends and traditions, which we are bombarded with on a daily basis and which so many people adopt without much comprehension or thought. It is these numerous trends and traditions that appear to be confusing the laymen in our various societies, for the truly essential and significant Islamic values seem to be getting continuously eclipsed by the less significant ones. Why? It is probably because the less significant are usually easier to notice and imitate; while, the significant ones are typically characterized by a nature requiring from the person stronger will-power and self-control. The case, for example, of dressing yourself in a particular way in belief of adhering to Islamic attire or growing your beard at a certain length or eating in a certain way etc., is much easier than the case of getting yourself to forgive someone for mistreating you- a value of true significance in Islam and for which evidence is found in many verses in the Quran, like: "*But indeed if any show patience and forgive, that would truly be an exercise of courageous will and resolution in the conduct of affairs*" (Ash-shura, 43) and the verse "*Hold to forgiveness; command what is right; But turn away from the ignorant*" (Al-a'raf, 199). Forgiving, as an action, requires more of you personally; for, you would probably need to put yourself in your wrongdoers' shoes, try to be understanding of why they did what they did, and find enough kindness in your heart not to hold a grudge against them and to accept them despite what they did to you. In other words, in the case of forgiving, you are required to have more of an Islamic character and examples falling in this same category include, but are not limited to, the following: refusing to stand silent and instead taking action in the face of injustice done to oneself or to others; willing to sacrifice of self for others; and treating others mercifully and respectfully regardless of whether you like them or not; etc.

Adopting the significant values of Islam (or any other religion as a matter of fact) requires more effort from the person than adopting the less significant ones. This should not be taken to mean that what is being referred to here as 'the less significant values' are simply to be thrown out the window; all that is being said is that they should not be adopted at the expense of the truly significant ones. Regrettably, this seems to be what is manifesting itself in many, if not all, Arab and Islamic societies. The main issue is to try and understand why this is happening. In other words, why- other than the reason that it is easier- are most people sticking to the less significant values and failing to adopt and act according to the more essential ones from which we derive our true Islamic ethics and character?

Taking into consideration an Aristotelian ethical perspective, the explanation of this phenomenon is as follows. As Aristotle would say, good character (like the true Islamic character in this context) is not something we are born with but rather something that we acquire through training and practice. It comes neither from indoctrination nor from simply mimicking the right or proper actions. Instead, it develops from getting trained in the repetition of the right types of practical reasoning in conjunction with the truly good values or- in this case- the significant Islamic values. What is meant by *practical reasoning* is deliberation to fulfill a rational desire for something believed to be good (Irwin, 1980). It is only when this thing that is believed to be good is *truly good* i.e. stemming from the right values- and not just appearing to be good but is not so in reality- that practical reasoning results in good or right actions (Gauthier, 1963). The repetition of this type of reasoning coupled with the right or significant values ultimately leads to the repetition of proper actions in the many different situations we encounter in our daily life and, thus, such repeated actions become habits that form the individual's character. Habituation aiming at the development of the good character, therefore, is not a 'mindless process' whereby the individual getting the training is simply imitating the person who is educating them; instead, what is deeply involved in the process of habituation is a kind of assessment of the situation that one is in, in addition to, a kind of 'seeing' or 'noticing' what is required in such a situation (Sorabji, 1980).

This type of training requires time, effort, and long-term monitoring on the part of the trainers, be it the parents, caregivers, schoolteachers, and/or religious *imams* (leaders), to ensure that the significant values coupled with the proper practical reasoning become habits in the individual trainee and thus constitute their Islamic character. With the considerably fast pace of life and with the hustle and bustle of our contemporary world, in addition to the numerous economic, financial, and security hassles we are forced to worry about in our Arab societies, not too many individuals are gaining in their households and surroundings this specific type of training. Why not? The answer simply is that most of those who are supposed to be doing the training are failing to fulfill their responsibility, mainly because of the reasons mentioned above but also because of ignorance in relation to what truly constitutes the true Islamic character. This ignorance is primarily due to the confusion resulting from their tendency to unconsciously and involuntarily fall into the trap of treading the easier path of imitation and indoctrination of the less significant values at the expense of the more significant ones.

One only needs to look around carefully, watch some Arabic talk shows, read a few newspapers, browse some of the Arabic websites, and communicate with various groups of people to find evidence for the state of confusion our Arab World is currently in on the religious, interpersonal, and ethical levels and to find proofs of unacceptable actions and behaviors resulting from this confusion. Stories of violations, mistreatment, deception, and abuse are plenty. No need for denial therefore. What we need instead is to stop being too harsh on ourselves by always pretending to be morally perfect societies and to admit our faults, in order to be able to correct them more effectively. It is about time for us to realize the confusion around us that is distancing us from our true Islamic character, which is in essence characterized by mercy and compassion. This distance is one of the causes leading to cases of violations and infringements as horrific and merciless as child abuse.

Combatting Passivity

The second step would be to get rid of some of our passivity in the face of cases of abuse. In some situations, our passivity is due in part to mere indifference and to being mainly engrossed in one's own concerns and issues. Most of the time, however, people's passivity in the religiously conservative social contexts is due to extreme reliance on *Allah* (God), to an extent that is really unacceptable by our religion. What is meant by extreme reliance here is dependence to the point that one does not act at all, in belief of leaving things as they are and waiting to see what *Allah* will bring or, in other words, just leaving things to *Allah's* mercy. This kind of attitude in reality contradicts the true principles of our religion; for, not doing anything or being silent in the face of injustice, for example, is as bad as taking part in it. Our religion demands of us to seek, pursue, and do what is good instead of standing still. It is only then that *Allah* stands by us and guides us. Or else, what would be the difference between us and, for instance, the two characters *(Vladimir and Estragon)* in Samuel Beckett's play *Waiting for Godot*? Those two characters stand doing absolutely nothing in the middle of an unknown road, not knowing where they've been or where they are heading. Their existence is meaningless and totally absurd and the only thing they do in life is wait for a mysterious rescuer named *Godot* to come and save them- *Godot* whom they are uncertain of when or whether he would even show up!

Islam is definitely way different in its outlook on humans than the picture portrayed in Beckett's play; for, from the beginning, man is born with a purpose in life, which is to surrender oneself to

6

Allah by worshipping and serving Him, simply through, thoughts, feelings, and actions that make us better creatures and that, as Al-Hayani (2007) states, lift humanity to a higher spiritual level. One of the central themes in the Quran is God's faith that humankind can and will achieve goodness on earth through the knowledge that He has bestowed no other creatures with (Al-Hayani, 2007). This knowledge is a responsibility and a trust to be applied to the betterment of mankind through the implementation of good deeds and the prevention of evil. Its application is a religious duty and an act of worship, for through it we can achieve righteousness, which is: the carrying out of God's work, the alleviation of hunger and suffering, the securing of equity and justice for everyone, the preservation of the natural balance in the world, and the abidance by God's sacred laws (Al-Hayani, 2007). Worship, therefore is not to be understood only as rituals of obeisance and adoration but also in the ways we as humans relate to one another, fostering harmony and mutual benefit to all (Mohammed, 2004). From the beginning, therefore, we have to first start with ourselves (developing, improving, changing, etc. ourselves). We are, in other words, required to *act* and then *Allah* steps in to guide and support us. Evidence for this is found in the Holy Quran in the following verse: *"Verily never will God change the condition of a people until they change it themselves" (Ar-ra`d, 11).*

Knowing therefore, for example, that your neighbor's or relative's or friend's children- or even your own- are being subject to any form of abuse and standing doing nothing but praying for them is something not acceptable according to the Islamic formula. For if you really want to see any change for the better in your *ummah* (community) and you truly care about being a good Muslim, it is a must that you do more. This is precisely the reason why this work was developed.

Chapter Two

The Three 'D's: Definitions, Dilemmas, and Data

For a sensible discussion of the topic of child abuse, it is imperative to have a clear understanding of the concept of children's rights and the definition of a 'child', as well as having an idea of what incidents are generally considered as cases of child abuse.

Definition of a Child and Related Concepts

According to the United Nations' Convention on the Rights of the Child (CRC), a 'child' is defined as a person below the age of 18, unless the relevant laws recognize an earlier age of majority. Generally, the concept of childhood is thought of as a straightforward and self-explanatory one; however, some scholars like Collings, S. and Davies, L. (2008) argue that when we talk about children, very often ideas about childhood are taken for granted, are emotionally resonant, and are differently understood from one cultural context to another. They have identified, through a study they conducted on child protection workers in Ontario, Canada, four main different discourses of childhood: (1) the child as vulnerable and innocent; (2) the child as an incomplete adult; (3) the child as a rights-bearing individual; and (4) the child as a social actor. The first discourse, which is the most pervasive one, views the child as pure, innocent, naturally good, and unequipped to manage the threats of the adult world, and thus is in need of protection and sheltering by responsible adults. The second one views the child as being in a state of becoming yet to be formed and developed into a future adult or citizen. This discourse implies that with proper guidance through education and other children services, a child may be rescued from undesirable economic, social, and cultural conditions. The third discourse is rooted in the modern notion of children as rights-bearing individuals, which developed after the 1982 adoption of the CRC. This discourse portrays the child as carrying sacred rights as individual-rights that are distinct from the family and the community one lives in. Finally, the fourth discourse affirms children's full human capacities in making decisions about their lives and this discourse is most evident in movements that target children's oppression and argue for children's voices to be heard. These discourses, as different as they may seem, tend to overlap and at times to even contradict each other. Still, they are important for one to be aware of in any discussion related to children's protection, in order to ensure clarity and consistency in terminology and meaning. If we look closely at the Arab World, the third and fourth discourses, i.e. respectively the child as a rights-bearing individual and as a social actor, seem to be almost nonexistent in it, except for maybe in a very few and elite circles.

In child welfare discussions, the two discourses that usually dominate, according to Collings and Davies (2008) are the child as vulnerable and in need of rescue and the child as a right-bearing individual. Viewing the child as holding human rights has some benefits to the protection of children, since this view takes into consideration the importance of guaranteeing children the same rights to security and dignity that adults have (Collings & Davies, 2008). According to the CRC, children everywhere have the following basic human rights: the right to survival; to develop to the fullest; to protection from harmful influences, abuse, and exploitation; and to participate fully in family, cultural, and social life. The four guiding principles of the Convention are non-discrimination; devotion to the best interests of the child; the right to life, survival, and development; and respect for the views of the child. These rights and principles are among the internationally accepted human rights of the United Nations. Despite the fact that the CRC focuses on universality, it also acknowledges that every culture has a specific image of childhood and, consequently, admits that within the cultural background, a child will have specific needs and rights (Mijnarends, 1993).

Examples of CRC Violations from the Arab World

Note that despite the fact that most Arab countries have ratified the CRC, a lot of its principles and laws are not actually enforced, as was discovered by many researchers in the Arab region and as, unfortunately, the conditions around us continue to indicate. In the Middle East, for example, child labor continues despite many laws prohibiting the practice and in Lebanon, in particular, laws requiring a minimum age for working children and compulsory education were- and still continue to be- usually ignored (Makhoul et al, 2004). In Jordan, despite the many attempts over the years to adapt the CRC to the country's context and despite some improvement, labor laws are still in many cases applied only to working children contracted by recognized industries; whereas, legislation is ineffective where conditions are the most hazardous, namely in the informal sectors and in the smaller enterprises (Hammad, 1999). There continues to be also in Jordan a lack of awareness and sensitization on child rights, the CRC, and the Jordanian Child Rights Law, as had been discovered by Hammad (1999). One major challenge existing there is that the private sphere is almost treated as sacred and so any intervention into family affairs in the name of children's rights continues to be most of the time highly resisted (Hammad, 1999). In other Arab countries, even Lebanon, which is one of the least conservative in the region, the same applies (Usta &Farver, 2010). In the United Arab Emirates (UAE), for example, open discussion of controversial issues such as child abuse, and especially sexual abuse, is not acceptable (Crabtree, 2008). In many societies in the Middle East and North Africa, child marriages are still common and very little has been done to combat this form of exploitation, despite the rising awareness of the harm associated with it (Mikhail, 2002). In these types of marriages, girls' consent is not taken and this is a clear violation of their rights according to not only several international declarations but also to Islamic law. In addition, a considerable percentage of these underage wives get beaten by their husbands (29% in Egypt; 26% in Jordan); not to forget that most if not all of them are forced into sexual relations, denied their freedom and personal development; and are prevented from continuing their education (Mikhail, 2002). Additionally, in some Arab countries and mainly the African ones like Somalia, Sudan, Mauritania, Egypt, and Djibouti, the percentages of little girls who undergo female genital mutilation, according to statistics from the United Nations Children's Fund (UNICEF), regrettably continue to be considerably high. "Female circumcision does not exist in the Quran and there is no evidence that the Prophet recommended it. In the Muslim areas where it is practiced, as in parts of northeastern Africa, it is the consequence of local pre-Islamic practices" (Mahdavi, 2008; n.p.).

Going back to Lebanon, there are almost no laws there protecting children from adult-inflicted violence, where violence in this case is defined as any act that negatively affects or can affect the health and welfare of a child; it may be physical, psychological, or verbal and may increase in severity if overlooked (Makhoul et al, 2004). In many parts of the Arab World, moreover, physical violence is viewed as an effective and normal child-rearing practice (Makhoul et al, 2004). It seems therefore that in many cases, there is a mix between what is considered as adult-inflicted violence which leads to child abuse or maltreatment, on the one hand, and verbal and physical discipline on the other. The two, however, are different: the former involves non-accidental injury, while the latter in the great majority of cases does not involve it (McKee et al, 2007). The latter, furthermore is implemented for purposes of correction or control, i.e. as an aspect of socialization (Straus & Paschall, 2009) whereas the former is usually a reaction to conditions of increased stress and scarcity of resources, such as low socioeconomic status or unemployment, or to increased family stress resulting from overcrowded conditions in big families or from health problems or from family conflicts etc. (Sadowski et al, 2004). In some cases also adult-inflicted violence results from adults whom themselves had experienced maltreatment as children (Sadowski et al, 2004).

Due to these existing differences, violence or abuse inflicted on a child should never be misinterpreted as a form of discipline, as it unfortunately is in many parts of our Arab World. This point is supported especially by the fact that some research studies have indicated that corporal punishment (by itself), like spanking or slapping a child, can adversely affect cognitive ability, cause children stress for several years, undermine the bond between the child and the parent, and reduce a child's motivation to learn from parents (Straus & Paschall, 2009). An extensive body of research also indicates that harsh discipline (physical alone or physical plus verbal) is associated with higher levels of child externalizing problems (like aggressive behavior, fighting with other children, stealing, etc.); while, harsh verbal discipline especially from the fathers is associated with higher levels of child internalizing problems (like feeling hopeless, worrying a lot, being withdrawn, etc.) (Mckee et al, 2007). If, therefore, simply spanking or slapping or yelling at a child could have such adverse effects, one can only imagine then what sort of effects adult-inflicted acts of violence, which usually result in injury to a child, could have.

The Controversial Case of Saudi Arabia

The above are just a few examples of how some of the principles and laws of the CRC are not actually enforced in the Arab countries that have ratified this convention. Note, furthermore, that despite the international recognition of human rights in general, some countries, like the Kingdom of Saudi Arabia for example, hold a noncompliant and controversial position towards some of those rights, especially the ones that are incompatible with the cultural values of Eastern states and simultaneously inconsistent with the Islamic *Shari'ah* (religious law, which is the supreme law in Saudi Arabia) (Al-Hargan, 2005). Saudi Arabia is actually faced with a major dilemma when confronted with some of the internationally accepted human rights. One such right is the right to change one's religious faith; for, Islamic *Shari'ah* forbids Muslims from changing their religion. Another right is that of non-discrimination on the basis of gender; for, Islamic *Shari'ah* gives Muslim males different rights to enjoy than Muslim females. For example, the weight given to the evidence provided by a man is greater than that given to the evidence provided by a woman; in terms of the right to inheritance, a woman is entitled to only half of what a man inherits even when she has an equal degree of relationship with the deceased individual; and a man is entitled to marry up to four wives at the same time but a woman is not allowed to marry without the permission of her guardian or a judge, who is always a man; etc. (Al-Hargan, 2005). A third right is that of non-discrimination on the basis of religion; for Islamic *Shari'ah* obliges non-Muslims living in Islamic states to pay a tax (*jizya*) for their security and for enjoying a limited freedom of religion- a tax that Muslims do not have to pay. Besides, in the cases of homicide or bodily harm, non-Muslims are entitled to a financial compensation *(diyyah)* that is only half of that payable to Muslims (Al-Hargan, 2005). Regardless of the justifications behind these Islamic principles and regardless of how they are viewed by the West, what in reality complicates the picture in the specific case of Saudi Arabia and any other country that is under the Islamic *Shari'ah* (law) is that there is a fundamental difference between the legal system of these countries and the Western legal systems, from which international human rights originated. In the Western legal systems, the sovereignty is with the people and the nation's representatives are entitled to change existing laws and to create new ones when necessary. While, under Islamic *Shari'ah*, God (*Allah*) alone is the sovereign and Muslims are to function and adjust their actions according to His law at all times. What this means is that the rights of Muslims are granted to them by the *Shari'ah* and by virtue of the divine will and not by virtue of being human beings as is perceived in the West (Al-Hargan, 2005). In addition, the path to human dignity in Islamic cultures is not through the protection of unalienable individual rights as in the West but rather through the performance of duties and obligations to society that is guided by Islamic law and in which a Muslim can best reach his or her full potential (Price, 2002). All of this infers that if a certain international human right is incompatible with the Islamic *Shari'ah*, there is absolutely no way that it could be accepted in societies that abide by such a legal system, simply because changes to what was willed by God are not permitted. The situation here therefore is not a matter of lack of enforcement of an international convention's principles and laws, as is the case in other Arab countries, but rather a matter of the unfeasibility of even ratifying some of them. This may explain a little the source of the current tension existing between a country like Saudi Arabia and the West in relation to the issue of human rights; for Saudi Arabia, which is commonly called `The Land of the Two Holy Mosques` in reference to Makkah and Al-Madinah, the two holiest Islamic cities, is- and more so than other Arab countries-constantly under attack by the West, accusing it of committing human right violations. The question however is this: are some of the human rights Saudi Arabia is being accused of violating ones that are considered universal by the West but are not perceived as rights in Saudi Arabia because they happen to contradict Islamic *Shari'ah*? If so, then no wonder that the tension exists at the scale it does, for what the West views as a violation, Muslims in Saudi Arabia perceive as an exercise of obedience to the divine will of God. Not only that, but for one community or nation to try and impose its perceived values upon another, as the case would be most probably interpreted here, would be considered by Muslims as tyranny, even if the imposition may take the appearance of the teaching of `human rights`(Mohammed 2004).

The case, therefore, that some Western scholars like Sifa Mtango (2004) try to make by claiming that every state has the responsibility of removing any inconsistency between international human rights law binding on it, on the one hand, and religious customary laws operating within its territories, on the other, cannot always hold because in part the situation seems to be, as we saw above, a matter of how things get interpreted and perceived. The issue, additionally, is not just a matter of things getting interpreted differently because of cultural particularities that play a decisive role in such interpretations; if it were, things would be much easier, since cultures are dynamic and their practices can always be adapted and reformed. In other words, the focal point here is not *culture* as much as it is *Shari'ah* i.e. *the expression of God's will*; the two are different in that the former is manmade and can be changed unlike the latter.

It is true that, in some cases and in certain Islamic contexts, disputes may happen over how certain aspects of *Shari'ah* are understood and over how they are to be applied, and abuses of *Shari'ah* do unfortunately happen by certain religious jurists; however, the fact remains that there are many aspects of it that are crystal clear and are expressed in an absolutely clear-cut manner in the Quran and some of them happen to be inconsistent with certain accepted international human rights. A simple example here would be the internationally accepted human right of equality between men and women and the total elimination of differences between them, on the one hand, and the Islamic right to inheritance, on the other, through which a woman is entitled to only half of what a man inherits. There is no ambiguity whatsoever in Islamic contexts about this right to inheritance and there is only one accepted interpretation of it and, thus, no claim could ever be made that a certain jurist is interpreting this aspect of *Shari'ah* in his own way just to subjugate a certain member of the female race; although, it is precisely Islamic principles like these that have led to a perceived Western view of Islam as undermining women's rights (Esposito, 2005). How can such an inconsistency between the two rights in question, therefore, be eradicated without the consideration of only one of them and the disregard of the other? It just cannot and requesting from an Islamic state like Saudi Arabia to disregard the right to inheritance as stated in the *Shari'ah* would be asking it to disobey the divine will of God. Because of its identity as the cradle of Islam and because of its place in the Islamic World, the Saudi state is simply not in a position to do such a thing. Certainly, however, when the case is such that a certain aspect of *Shari'ah* may be interpreted in more than one way, then it can be argued that states fully operating under *Shari'ah* legal systems need to take into account internationally accepted human rights and reconciliation should be reached. One way to shorten the distance toward such reconciliations is the suggestion supported by Muslim scholars like Fazlur Rahman and Khaleel Mohammed (2004), which is for Muslims to try and understand the text in the Quran and the *Shari'ah* aspects rooted in it, in terms of what it meant in its historical time and then to try and infer from it a philosophy that is more applicable to our modern world. At the same time, as Beverly Dawn Metcalfe (2007) points out, the West needs to learn to appreciate the dominance of religion on the Arab individual life and if individuals in a Muslim state are treated differently whether gender-wise or else, the differences should not always automatically be linked to ideas of subordination and deference. This is especially true since even though not all Arab countries apply the entire code of Islamic *Shari'ah*, most of them adopt at least a few aspects of it and, in all of them, family law and what is known as the personal status law are derived from and governed by Islamic *Shari'ah*. Even in the complicated case of Lebanon- which has 17 official religious sects, each with its own family law and religious courts- Muslim courts are governed by *Shari'ah* law based on the different juristic schools they adopt. Religion, therefore, is a significant impacting factor on the Arab individual and their life and it should not, as a result, be taken lightly.

A note of clarification is needed at this point in relation to the preceding argument made: it was not intended in any way to undermine the internationally accepted human rights. Nor was it intended as a justification of actual human right violations that do occur in Saudi Arabia or any other country functioning fully under Islamic *Shari'ah* legal system. In brief, it was only meant as an attempt to try and explain only one of the possible causes behind the existing tension between the religiously strict Islamic countries and the West and, also, to reveal that the situation is not as simplistic as one may assume it to be.

The positive thing that remains is that, despite the incompatibility existing between the Islamic *Shari'ah* and some of the human rights that are accepted internationally, when it comes down to the rights of the child as spelled out by CRC, Islamic values are completely consistent with these rights and principles. For this reason, even a country like Saudi Arabia, which is completely ruled by Islamic *Shari'ah*, signed and ratified the CRC in 1996 and child abuse and neglect were recognized at major health facilities throughout the country by the end of the decade (Al Eissa & Almuneef, 2010). It is even widely argued that children rights and principles even existed way back before the introduction of any international convention (Hammad, 1999).

Consistency Between CRC Principles and Islam

Islam, in fact, put an end to major human rights violations that were widely practiced in the Arabian Peninsula, before its inception and prevalence as a religion (i.e. during the time known as *al-jahiliyya*) (Al-Mahroos et al, 2005). One such violation- which relates in particular to a child's right to life- is that of female infanticide, which was clearly prohibited in one of the Holy Quran's verses in *Al-nah'l*. The Quran, in addition, describes children as one of the 'allurements or ornaments of life' that make the life of this world more beautiful and worthy (*Al-kahf* 18: 46) and rights, according to Prophet Muhammad's teachings *(Peace be upon him)*, "...should be granted the child even before conception: Muslims are urged to select a spouse that can ensure a healthy, secure, and pious upbringing for the child" (Hammad, 1999, p.218). It is the obligation, therefore, of every Muslim to not accept any condition or factor that may act as a threat to, or as an abuse or neglect of, a child's right to health or safety or general well-being.

Definitions and Forms of Abuse and Neglect

Speaking of abuse and neglect, it is necessary to see exactly how these concepts are commonly defined. Although there are some researchers (Fakunmoju, Bammeke, Bosiakoh, Asante, Wooten, Hill, and Karpman, 2013) who argue for the need to take into consideration cultural differences in perception of maltreatment and what practices constitute it, some behaviors continue to be universally deemed as abusive. Based on the 2008 recommendation of the American Psychological Association (APA) in preparation for the Child Abuse Prevention and Treatment Act (CAPTA) of the U.S. House of Representatives, and as mentioned on the APA official website, the term 'child abuse' means the following:

> "...Any act or failure to act on the part of a parent or other person responsible for the child's care, which causes or has the potential to cause death, physical or emotional harm or impairment, sexual abuse or exploitation, or endangerment of the child's health or safety."

While 'neglect' is defined by the APA as follows:

> "...At a minimum, the failure of a person having the care or custody of a child to provide adequate food, clothing, shelter, medical care, or supervision where no physical injury to the child has occurred but where the child's physical or mental health, welfare, or safety may be at risk."

The typical forms of child abuse and neglect that are considered as child maltreatment are: physical abuse, emotional abuse, sexual abuse, physical neglect, and emotional neglect (Polonko, 2006). All these forms "...are associated with devastating consequences for children and the adults they become" (Polonko, 2006: 266).

The consequences or effects of child maltreatment will be discussed in detail later on in this work; now, however, it is important to look at the scope of child maltreatment, which is large to the extent that violations of children's rights to protection take place in every country and are massive (Takrouri, 2007). Actually, maltreatment in the form of child abuse and neglect has been one of the most common and yet unrecognized and ignored phenomena affecting children around the world (WHO & ISPCAN, 2006). Such violations do not only take place in underdeveloped societies as is often assumed but also in rich nations. Actually, in 2007, the UNICEF published a report on child well-being which showed major nations like the UK and the USA at the bottom of a league of 21 rich countries with respect to the well-being of their children (Takrouri, 2007). Child maltreatment, additionally, does not only happen in the child's home; it also takes place in organizations involving children, like schools, child care businesses, government agencies, churches, etc. It can also happen almost anywhere like in cases of kidnapping, random murders, etc. and it usually is far more common in single-parent families than in families with both parents (Takrouri, 2007). The industrious societies with their well-organized media often focus attention on certain cases of abuse, making them appear so prominent; while in remote areas outside of the scope of such media attention, there may be more horrific cases of maltreatment that are not revealed and related stories that are not covered (Halwani, 2008). In the Arab countries and in particular in the Middle East, since the issue of child abuse is somewhat a taboo topic of discussion (Takrouri, 2007), many cases stay unrevealed to the public and such type of evidence for children in Arab countries is so little. This constitutes a major area of concern since these countries, based on the United Nations 2009 demographic profile of them, have a total population of 353 million, of whom approximately

34% are under the age of 15. If we take, for instance, the case of the Arabian Gulf region in specific, we will easily realize that child abuse reports began to appear in the medical literature only after the 1980s (Al-Mahroos et al, 2005). In Saudi Arabia, for example, there were only 11 reports published in the medical literature from 1990 to 2000 and all were case studies (Al Eissa & Almuneef, 2010). Till this day, the number of such reports in the region remains quite limited, despite a noticeable increase in recognition and reporting of child abuse by both families and professionals, due to cultural changes and public awareness about such incidents (Al Eissa & Almuneef, 2010). The research project done by Al-Mahroos et al in 2005 on Bahraini children probably remains to be one of the studies reporting the largest number of abused children from this region. The study included 150 abused children who were referred to the Child Protection Committee of the Salmaniya Medical Complex from June 1991 to July 2001. The majority of these children had been sexually abused; some were physically abused; and a few were both sexually and physically abused. Only 3 cases were ones of neglect.

Statistical Data from the Arab World

With little research reports to shed light on the scope of child maltreatment in the Arab World, one would think that the best resort would be to look at related statistics from UNICEF. The ChildInfo web pages of UNICEF provide statistics on child protection by country for a number of categories, some of which are: child labor, child marriage, child violent discipline, and female genital mutilation (FGM). Child labor is defined by UNICEF as work that goes beyond a minimum number of hours, depending on the age of the child and on the nature of the work; while child marriage is the union of a woman with a man before she reaches the age of 18. Violent discipline, according to UNICEF, is any action taken by a parent or a caregiver that is meant to cause a child physical or emotional pain, in order to correct behavior and act as a deterrent. Last but not least, female genital mutilation is described by both UNICEF and the World Health Organization (WHO) as ``the partial or total removal of the female external genitalia or other injury to the female genital organs for cultural or other non-therapeutic reasons"(UNICEF official website). Despite the statistics provided by UNICEF, however, a problem remains since data are not available for all categories from every Arab country. For example, no statistics are available from Jordan, Kuwait, Libya, the Occupied Palestinian Territories and the Gaza Strip, Oman, Qatar, Saudi Arabia, Tunisia, and the UAE for the category of child labor. No statistics are available from Bahrain, Kuwait, Libya, Oman, Qatar, Saudi Arabia, and the United Arab Emirates (UAE) for the category of child marriage. As regards, violent discipline of children, data is available from only seven of the twenty-two Arab countries, which are: Algeria, Djibouti, Egypt, Iraq, the Occupied Palestinian Territories, Syria, and Yemen; while concerning female genital mutilation, statistics are available from only six countries, which are Djibouti, Egypt, Mauritania, Somalia, Sudan, and Yemen. Note that lack of available statistics from some Arab countries in no way indicates absence of such types of child maltreatment in their societies. What they do indicate, however, is a serious condition because with their deficiency and with the scarcity of related research reports, it is extremely difficult to tell how prevalent the phenomenon of child maltreatment is in these societies and, thus, equally difficult to set up plans for addressing it.

In any case, what can be concluded from the latest available UNICEF statistics is that the percentages of children aged 2-14 who experience any type of violent discipline are extremely high in the Arab countries from which data is collected. These countries are: Algeria, Djibouti, Egypt, Iraq, Lebanon, Morocco, State of Palestine, Syrian Arab Republic, and Yemen. Speaking more specifically and based on the latest data collected in the years 2005 to 2011, these percentages range from 72% to 95%, with Yemen and the State of Palestine ranking the highest on the list and Djibouti ranking lowest, although still with a considerably high percentage of 72. As regards child labor, the percentages of children aged 5-14 engaged in any of its forms in Algeria, Bahrain, Comoros, Djibouti, Egypt, Iraq, Jordan, Lebanon, Mauritania, Morocco, Somalia, Sudan and South Sudan, Syrian Arabic Republic, and Yemen range, based on statistics from 2002 to 2011, from 2% to 49%, with Jordan and Lebanon ranking lowest on the list and Somalia ranking highest. For the category of child marriage, the percentages of women aged 20-24, who were married before the age of 18 in the countries for which data is available (Algeria, Djibouti, Egypt, Iraq, Jordan, Lebanon, Mauritania, Morocco, Somalia, State of Palestine, Syrian Arab Republic, and Yemen), range, according to statistics from the years 2000-2011, from 2% to 45%, with Algeria ranking lowest on the list and Somalia ranking highest. In relation to female genital mutilation, the percentages of women aged 15-49 with at least one daughter circumcised in the countries for which data is available (Djibouti, Egypt, Mauritania, Somalia, and Yemen), range, according to data collected in the years 2002-2011, from 20% to 66%, with Yemen ranking lowest on the list and Mauritania ranking highest. While, the percentages of women aged 15-49 who themselves had been circumcised range in the same countries and based on statistics from the same years, from 23% to 98%, with Yemen ranking lowest and Somalia ranking highest.

With the limited data available and with some of the significantly high percentages recorded above, it is safe to conclude that child maltreatment is a fact in the Arab World and is something to be taken seriously. It is present in many forms and cannot be ignored if the physical and mental integrity of children is to be maintained. Another equally important form of child maltreatment that cannot be ignored and which is, unfortunately, not included among UNICEF's different statistical categories is what is usually called *parental alienation*. This type of child maltreatment is very often overlooked and since it deserves serious attention, it will be extensively touched upon in one of the subsequent chapters of this book. Before that, however, it is important to take a closer look at the main causes behind child maltreatment and also at its short-term and long-term effects on children sufferers.

Chapter Three

Causes and Effects

Impact of Abuse and Neglect on Children

Despite a number of child protection initiatives in the Arab World, child maltreatment continues to be a serious problem for so many of our children, with profoundly detrimental results not only for the children themselves but also for society at large. To begin with, the association between child maltreatment and adverse physical and mental health outcomes is well established in a number of research documents (Springer et al, 2003). What research consistently demonstrates is that the adverse outcomes persist long after the maltreatment has stopped, often lasting throughout the individual's lifetime (Veltkamp et al, 1994). These outcomes are also usually more severe when children experience more than one type of child maltreatment, in contrast to experiencing only one type (Polonko, 2006). In addition, the consequences for children exposed to abuse or neglect are usually more or less the same regardless of culture: in brief, they are all children "...with a low self-esteem, a low opinion of the world, and social and psychological isolation; victims who move to take up defender behaviors" (Mijnarends, 1993: 215). They are also all at risk of one or more of the following: poor physical and mental health, educational problems, displacement, homelessness, and poor parenting skills later in life (Halwani, 2008), in addition to other possible adverse outcomes, including death. How a particular child gets affected by a certain form of maltreatment depends on a number of factors working in parallel at different levels or systems- factors like the child's own attributes, his or her family context, and aspects of the maltreatment he or she is subjected to (Glaser, 2000).

As mentioned previously in this work, child maltreatment comes in different forms, which can all be broadly categorized under two main types: child abuse and child neglect. Abuse can be physical or emotional or sexual; while neglect can be either physical or emotional. In some unfortunate cases, of course, the neglect can be both physical and emotional and the abuse can be a combination of any two of its three forms or even all the three together. Additionally, it is not infrequent that abuse and neglect coexist in some cases. Both abuse and neglect, especially in the early years, have the potential to affect subsequent brain functioning and this is mainly because both of them are potent sources of stress (Glaser, 2000), which has adverse effects on brain development and specifically on the hippocampus that is integrally concerned with memory (Squire, 1992). Both of them can also contribute to the development of behavioral and emotional difficulties in children (Al-Krenawi et al, 2007).

With respect to neglect, researchers like Erickson and Egeland (2002) have discovered that the physical kind is the most widely recognized and commonly studied of its forms. It "includes failure to protect from harm or danger and provide for the child's basic physical needs, including adequate shelter, food, or clothing" (Erikson & Egeland, 2002:6); while, emotional neglect includes the inattention of the caregivers to the child's emotional needs, nurturing, or emotional well-being. Although emotional neglect is less obvious than the physical one, it is another commonly studied type of child neglect and can still have serious long-term consequences on the child (Polonko, 2006). Other forms of neglect that have not received as much attention from researchers are prenatal neglect and financial neglect. The former refers to "the parent's failure to obtain adequate pre and postnatal care deemed necessary for the physical, neurological and cognitive development of the fetus and neonate; "while, the latter refers to "failure to provide economically for one's children" (Polonko, 2006: 262-263). Both types are associated with grave consequences for the child.

If we look closely at the consequences of child neglect, we notice that the physical type has the most destructive outcomes of any maltreatment types on a child's IQ, cognitive development, grades, and educational attainment later in life. It is also associated with considerably increased aggression and violent behavior, although less so than physical abuse (Polonko, 2006). Emotional neglect, on the other hand, does not seem to highly affect grades or IQ but is associated with significantly higher levels of psychopathology, i.e. the development of psychiatric disorders- a similarity it shares with child physical, sexual, and emotional abuse. In specific, emotionally neglected children are usually found to be socially withdrawn, inattentive, and aggressive (Glaser, 2000), in addition to being at risk of social rejection and pervasive feelings of incompetence (Finzi et al, 2000) as well as developing character and personality disorders (Polonko, 2006).

In relation to types of abuse, physical abuse seems to be the one with the most devastating consequences, since it's been found to be associated the most with low self-esteem, character disorders, aggression, violent behavior, and heavy drug use (Polonko, 2006). This is in addition to its association with a high incidence of post-traumatic stress disorder (PTSD) (Bremner et al, 1993), which is especially common in children and adolescents who have experienced high interpersonal intensity traumas (Donnely & Amaya-Jackson, 2002) such as physical and/or sexual abuse. The main features of PTSD include, in addition to experiencing or witnessing a traumatic or life-threatening event or one that involves threat or injury to oneself or others, re-experiencing the trauma, avoidance behavior, and hyperarousal. In other words, after the trauma, a child may have intrusive memories or sudden flashbacks associated with the traumatic experience; avoid stimuli like thoughts and feelings related to it and even refuse to acknowledge or discuss its occurrence; and suffer from sleep disturbance, irritability, anger outbursts, concentration problems, and even hypervigilance, which is ``a persistent agitation involving scanning of the environment for danger" or an exaggerated startle reaction (Donnelly & Amaya-Jackson, 2002: 160). Children with PTSD may have persistent symptoms that interfere with their development (Mcleer et al, 1988) like: repeated nightmares, fears including fear of the dark or specific fears related to their abuse, in addition to visions of the trauma that are sometimes considered by the parents or the teachers as excessive daydreaming on the part of the child (Graham, 1993). These children and adolescents also usually have at least one comorbid disorder, like attention deficit hyperactivity disorder (ADHD), including hyperactivity, impulsivity, restlessness, irritability, and distractibility (Cuffe et al, 1994) or more serious externalizing disorders like conduct disorder (CD) and oppositional defiant disorder (ODD) (Donnelly & Amaya-Jackson, 2002). Child physical abuse, moreover, has been for some time now recognized as one important risk factor for parenting, i.e. an important risk factor in the abuse of one's own children (Widom, 1989); although, this is not an inevitable outcome (Langeland & Dijkstra, 1995). This type of abuse has also been associated with poor academic achievement and this is due to the fact that children, who live with abusive parents, live in fear and use all their energy on trying to cope with the high levels of anxiety in their surroundings, instead of using it for concentrating on their learning tasks (Romeo, 2000). The end result for these children, eventually, is the achievement of poor grades, which in turn increases their risk of being abused again by their abusive parents in reaction to their underachievement (Romeo, 2000). Undesirable consequences other than these may also be present; however, what especially complicates matters in cases of physical abuse is the fact that, during interviews targeted at gathering information about the effects of such maltreatment or any other related information, child victims of such type of abuse are usually far less informative and responsive than victims of other forms of maltreatment (Lamb, 1999). Extracting information from such child victims is therefore an extremely challenging task.

As regards sexual abuse, it is regarded among the gravest threats to children's well-being and safety (Aboul-Hagag & Hamed, 2012). Most studies have found that its prevalence rates are higher for females than males (Aboul-Hagag & Hamed, 2012) and it is associated with a significantly high risk of developing anxiety disorders, major depressive disorders, alcohol abuse, drug abuse, and antisocial behavior (Becker-Weidman & Hughes, 2008). This is in addition to having, as its long-term adverse consequence, the increased risk of facing difficulties in intimate interpersonal relationships (Fleming et al, 1999), as well as, the increased risk of sexual revictimization in adolescence and adulthood (Messman & Long, 1996; Muehlenhard et al, 1998). In other words, as consistently indicated by research, women who had been sexually abused in childhood are sexually assaulted in adulthood significantly more often than women who had never been sexually abused; they are also more likely as adults to be victims of marital violence (Jankowski et al, 2002). There are several theoretical models that try to explain this increased risk of revictimization. One of them for example identifies intrapersonal, interpersonal, and sociocultural factors that contribute to it, like: self-blame, poor recognition of risk, impaired self-image and self-efficacy, feelings of betrayal, and posttraumatic stress symptoms (Jankowski et al, 2002).

Finally, when it comes to emotional abuse, the consequences are extremely damaging to the child. For example, verbal abuse has been often linked in the literature with poor educational outcomes, like: low test scores, poor classroom attendance, and an increase of placements in special education programs (Springer et al, 2003). Psychological aggression (i.e. yelling, cursing, threatening, or name calling) as well as psychological maltreatment (i.e. scorning, terrorizing, isolating, exploiting, and denying emotional responsiveness) have been both associated with developmental and adjustment problems (Gagne et al, 2007), as well as with eating disorders and mental health problems in adulthood (Glaser, 2000).

The main outcomes or effects of child maltreatment outlined above constitute a serious problem for so many children and can have negative repercussions for society at large; since, the prosperity of a certain society stems from the health and productivity of the individuals of which it is comprised. A society with adults who have a history of abuse and/ or neglect can only have limited prosperity because of all the physical and mental challenges these individuals are faced with, as a result of the maltreatment they were subjected to as children- challenges such as maladjustment, depression, low self-esteem, social isolation and withdrawal, educational problems, aggression, antisocial behavior, etc. In brief, therefore, child abuse and neglect are, as Glaser (2000) puts it, (wo)man-made phenomena that adversely affect children's development and sometimes survival. Not only that but they also negatively affect society as a whole and should, at least in theory, be preventable. On the practical level, on the other hand, they should be combated in all possible ways.

Factors Leading to Child Maltreatment

With the main outcomes or effects of child abuse and neglect outlined above, it is now time to shift attention to the possible causes or factors that place children at risk of maltreatment. It is important to mention here that there is relatively little research on such factors and, in particular, research that relates to the characteristics of the parents who abuse and/or neglect their children. The reason for the scarcity of such research is mainly the fear of the parents themselves of being somehow accused or blamed for the maltreatment (Polonko, 2006). In any case, parents who neglect or abuse their children are usually ones whom themselves had experienced maltreatment in childhood (Sadowski et al, 2004). There tends to be therefore what some researchers (Pianta et al, 1989:243 and Polansky et al, 1981:43) have called an *"intergenerational cycle of neglect or violence"* wherein child neglect or abuse are passed down from one generation to the other. This cycle is only one of the factors that place children at the risk of maltreatment. Another factor, which places them at risk of neglect in specific, is that of them having parents characterized by the following, as indicated by several research studies (Chaffin et al, 1996; Dong et al, 2004; Dube et al, 2001; Pianta et al, 1989; Polansky et al, 1981; Widom, 1999; and Wolfe, 1985): low IQ and educational attainment; high rates of mental illness or character disorders; high levels of anxiety, aggressiveness, and defensiveness prenatally, before the child's birth; substance abuse of alcohol and drugs; use of arbitrary, inconsistent, and highly punitive discipline; etc. Another important factor linked with child neglect, as well as with child abuse, is maternal postpartum depression. A study by Weinberg and Tronick (1998) on the effects of emotional deprivation and insensitive-intrusive care on children's development yielded results that indicated a compromise of development in an infant's cognitive, behavioural, and emotional functioning. These effects lasted beyond the mother's depression and beyond her resumption of normal interaction with the infant (Glaser, 2000). Finally, other major factors placing children at risk are the parents' reactions to conditions of increased stress and scarcity of resources, such as low socioeconomic status or unemployment, or to increased family stress resulting from overcrowded conditions in big families or from health problems or from family conflicts etc. (Sadowski et al, 2004). One factor that has not been paid as much attention to and which increases the risk of children being maltreated and, in particular, abused is that of bringing home a bad report card. One explanation for this is that many parents view their children as psychological extensions of themselves and interpret their children's poor report card grades as a reflection of their own personal inadequacies and failures (Romeo, 2000).

Children of Maltreatment Not Doomed to Failure

The causes and effects outlined above are the result of research studies conducted mainly in Western societies. In spite of this, it is safe to assume that the findings of these studies would be more or less similar to research results of cases of maltreated children in the Arab World. This is mainly because humans, in general, regardless of culture or society, have been endowed by human nature with some universal psychological processes that help them in addressing the problems of living (Matsumoto, 2007). These psychological processes include cognitive and emotional abilities as well as certain dispositions and preferences that make humans share similar behaviors and reactions across cultures. Children, whether Western or Arab, will therefore have relatively similar reactions to- i.e. will be affected in more or less similar ways by- life or survival threatening events such as abuse and neglect. This being said, the causes and effects outlined above may seem to draw an extremely gloomy picture for maltreated children. The good news though is that an abused child is not doomed to failure; for "if a child and his family have available and can participate in several well-conceived and administered intervention opportunities, a child's prospect for healthy psychological growth is enhanced"(Cupoli & Newberger, 1977: 312). Intervention opportunities, such as these, involve first, as the CRC endorses, extending to children the rights of human beings *(like the right to self-determination and the right to develop as an autonomous human being)* and second, challenging the belief systems and laws that support the power and privilege parents have to neglect and harm their children (Polonko, 2006 & Mijnarends, 1993). As Perry (1997:14) expresses it, "...we need to change the malignant and destructive view that children are the property of their biological parents. Children *belong* to the community, they are *entrusted* to parents." Parents, therefore, should not look at childhood as an isolated period where they decide what is good for the child; rather, they should view children as having opinions and should respect their ideas and wishes

(Mijnarends, 1993). This attempt at changing the destructive view of children as their parents' property should be accompanied in any intervention opportunity with the establishment of a true nurturing and support system not only for the maltreated children, but also for the parents who had been neglected or abused in childhood (Polonko, 2006).

The problem, however, is that well-conceived intervention opportunities, as described above, are not sufficiently available in all societies and, where available, they are not always responded to positively by some cultures. As we noted before, the mere discussion of issues such as child maltreatment is still considered as a taboo in many Arab World countries; convincing any Arab family, therefore, to take advantage of such intervention opportunities is no easy task, if at all possible. In addition, compulsory laws that can force the abusive parents to participate in such intervention opportunities are till now almost nonexistent. Besides, any intervention may be easily misconstrued as intrusion in one's personal family matters. The question that begs itself here, thus, is this: How can a detrimental phenomenon such as child maltreatment be at least curbed among the Arab populations, if not completely prevented?

What may instead work better and more easily than interventions in the Arab societies, and especially the predominantly Muslim ones, is what can be called *a process of reverting back to religion* and precisely *to the authentic Islamic values*. Islam, in general, plays a significant role in the cultural make-up of nations since it shapes both the spiritual and material spheres in life (Tayeb, 1997). In other words, in the predominantly Islamic countries, Islamic values are usually embedded in all aspects of civil society: individuals and state (Ahmed, 1998). This is why it is usually said that Islam is not only a *binding religion* but is also a *way of life*; for Islam is an all-embracing concept that represents both a human's relationship to God (*Allah*) and also a program of life (Ahmed, 1998). The significance of Islam is that it is a social and an organizing principle and its Quran and *Hadith* (Prophet Muhammad's teachings- *Peace be upon him*) provide a moral framework that will achieve the 'well-being' (*al-falah*) of all human beings (Ali, 1995; Ali et al, 2003). This being said, it is extremely important, therefore, as Metcalfe (2007, p.70) maintains "to appreciate the dominance of religion on the Arab individual life."

The role and power of Islam in a Muslim's life, as a result, should not be underestimated and the important fact that should be acknowledged is that the majority of Muslims, if not all, are more bound to their religion than to, let's say, some international convention such as CRC- which in any case, if one looks close enough, already has its primary principles embedded in the authentic Islamic values. The subsequent chapter provides evidence of how Islam already endorses each of the CRC principles.

Chapter Four

CRC Principles Embedded In Islamic Values

This section of the book has a clear objective, which as stated in the earlier chapter, is to provide evidence of how the primary principles of CRC are already embedded in Islamic values and how Islam already endorses each of these principles.

1. *CRC Principle of Non-Discrimination and Respect of the Child*

The Quran has given Muslims the mission to create a just and decent society in which all individuals, whether adults or children, are treated with respect (Armstrong, 2006). Muslims are expected to direct all their efforts and energies "...toward regulating the affairs of this world in the manner which God wants them to be regulated so that the universal standard of rule of law, justice, equality, peace, harmony, security, prosperity, and so on are guaranteed for the well-being of humankind" (Ali, 2005). There is no difference between how an adult and a child should be treated; even a child with disabilities or in need should not be discriminated against and, according to Islamic principles, should be provided with care and support from everyone in the family and society and not just predominantly from the mothers, as is usually the case in many Arab countries (Crabtree, 2007). Actually, the holy Quran requires Muslims to lend additional support to individuals who are considered more vulnerable, like women, children, orphans, refugees, and the needy, regardless of their faith or religion (Rahaei, 2012). Some practical Islamic concepts that are relevant in this context and which are highly praised as human actions are: *ihsan* (compassion), *ikram* (respect), and *eiwa'a* (full support). There are several verses in the Quran that call for *ihsan* by stressing that "all those who are in dire straits, particularly children, should be treated compassionately both in word and deed" (Rahaei, 2012; 4). Among these verses are: *Al-baqara* (83), *An-nisa'a* (36), and *Al-israa* (26). Similarly, there are several verses that call for *ikram* by emphasizing that "the needs of children and the needy should be met respectfully, in a way conforming to human dignity. Respect for children and efforts to meet their needs are a divine requirement" (Rahaei, 2012; 4). The most prominent of these verses is *Al-fajr* (17 and 18) in which it is made clear that God restricts a people's subsistence when they fail to honor the orphans and to encourage one another to feed the poor. Finally, as for *eiwa'a*, the verses in the Quran are many and all stress that "children, especially migrant children and those who have no caregivers, should be offered shelter and protection without expecting anything in return. Not paying attention to these children constitutes a failure in practice to comply with Islamic regulations" (Rahaei, 2012; 4). Some of these verses are *Ad-dhuha* (6 and 10); *An-nur* (22); *Al-ma'un* (1-7); and *Al-baqara* (177).

2. CRC Principle of a Child's Right to Protection from Harm, Abuse, and Exploitation

Muslims are ordered in the Quran and precisely in *surat Ad-dhuha* (i.e., *Ad-dhuha* chapter) to refuse to inflict any kind of pain, whether neglect or hunger or oppression, on others among them children and, especially, the orphans and the deprived. In fact, Muslims are required to imitate *Allah* (God) in all their dealings, i.e. they are to behave like Him and spread over others the wings of tenderness regardless of whom they are, whether adults or children (Armstrong, 2006).

Even though there are certain examples from *Hadith* and the Quran that have been frequently misinterpreted to mean the sanctioning of beating a child or a woman, there is sufficient reason to argue that in Islam inflicting any kind of pain or harm is prohibited. One such frequently misinterpreted example is the Quranic verse *An-nisa'a* (34), which states,

> Men are the protectors and maintainers of women, because God has given the one more (strength) than the other, and because they support them from their means. Therefore the righteous women are devoutly obedient, and guard in (the husband's) absence what God would have them guard. As to those women on whose part ye fear disloyalty and ill-conduct, admonish them (first), (Next), refuse to share their beds, (And last) beat them (lightly); but if they return to obedience, seek not against them Means (of annoyance): For God is Most High, great (above you all).

There is also the well-known *Hadith* of Prophet Muhammad (*Peace be upon him*), "Teach your children to pray when they are seven years old, and smack them if they do not do so when they are ten, and separate them in their beds." Both examples have been misinterpreted to mean, not only by Muslim laymen but also by traditional scholars, the sanctioning of beating. Nevertheless, since the Prophet (*Peace be upon him*) is considered to be within the traditional boundaries of Islamic scholarship "the perfect embodiment of the Quran's guidance" (Silvers, 2008), he should then be the ultimate human role model for any Muslim. What this means is that his behavior and actions are the example to be followed in everything in life. One cannot be a Muslim and accept Muhammad as Allah's prophet without accepting this basic premise. It follows, therefore, that there is a necessity to examine how the Prophet (*Peace be upon him*) behaved when the *An-nisa'a* (34) verse was revealed to him and then to try to imitate such behavior in similar instances or conditions. What is well-known, as Silvers (2008) explains and based on a number of works by

Muslim scholars, is that when this particular verse was revealed to him, he found himself in a dilemma over its meaning and had to painfully struggle with his conscience; for, the revelation seemed to be prescribing the beating of women in certain conditions, while he himself never hit his wives despite the possibility of those same conditions being present. Actually, it is reported that at the time the verse was revealed to him, he was uncomfortable even reciting it. Some argue that this feeling of discomfort may have been due to a previous exceptional experience that he had had with his wife Aisha (*God's blessings be upon her*), most likely before the revelation of the verse. This solitary experience was that of slapping or pushing Aisha in the chest when he caught her spying on him. It is safe to argue that from that experience, he had arrived at the conclusion that it is never acceptable to hit anyone at all and for this reason, he painfully struggled with the revelation of the verse. The fact that the Prophet (*Peace be upon him*) had a sincere struggle of conscience has led some Muslim scholars like Ibn Al-Arabi to conclude a valuable lesson from this example, basically that although we cannot deny any prescription in the holy Quran, we may still "...limit its practice to the point of complete prohibition in law and in our own ethical confrontation with the comprehensive possibilities of the Book, the world, and ourselves" (Silvers, 2008; 177). On the same lines, Silvers (2008) points out that the whole purpose of the verse's existence seems to be "...to inspire the crisis of conscience that would lead us to prohibit beating" (p.177) and the Prophet's example (*Peace be upon him*) "...shows us that there is no possible way to properly hit a woman" (p.177).

We argue here that if the Prophet's example (*Peace be upon him*) indicates that there is no possible way to properly hit a woman, then there can be no possible way either to properly hit whom is even more vulnerable and weaker, i.e. a child. So even if the *Hadith* stated above does mention the smacking of a child at the age of 10 for not performing prayer, it could not have meant the type of act that would inflict injury or harm on the child. For this reason, a lot of Muslim scholars stressed in their interpretation of this *Hadith* that hitting was to be used as a last resort, when disciplining a child over crucial matters, and it was to be used with rarity and with the satisfaction of two main conditions: (1) never to hit a child when angry and (2) to pay careful attention to how you are hitting, where you are hitting, and how much you are hitting, in order to ensure the safety of the child being disciplined. In other words, when disciplining a child, you have to make sure, as the Prophet *(Peace be upon him)* stated in one of his famous *Hadith,* to *"Observe justice in dealing with your children in the same manner in which you expect them to observe justice in being kind and good to you".* The relationship is mutual between the parents and the child and so needs to be one built on mercy, above all things, and needs to be a sample of the great loving and merciful relationship the Prophet *(Peace be upon him)* had with his own children, grandchildren, and children and people of the world; for he was above all else, as the Quran proclaims him to be in Verse *Al-anbiyaa* (107), "...a source of mercy to all the worlds" (Safi, 2009; 36).

3. CRC Principle of a Child's Right to Life, Survival, and Development

Probably the best proof of this principle's endorsement in the Quran is found in the following verse, which explicitly forbids the killing of children: *" Kill not your children for fear of want: We shall provide sustenance for them as well as for you. Verily the killing of them is a great sin" (Al-israa, 31).* This is in addition to the prohibition of female infanticide in the *surat Al-nah'l (Al-nah'l* chapter) of the Quran. While, with respect to the endorsement of a child's right to not only survival but also to healthy physical and emotional development, there is in the Quran evidence affirming the persistence of symbiosis between mother and child following birth through the infant's need for breast milk and it's mother's ability to provide it (Kocturk, 2003). For, at the time when the Quran was revealed, the civilizations of the eastern Mediterranean basin had already discovered the value of breast milk for an infant (Kocturk, 2003) and the holy Quran's recommendation in *surat Al-baqara* (i.e., *Al-baqara* chapter) of infants being breastfed for two whole years is proof of Islam's strong insistence on children's health and development. Not only that, but Islam also gave a child's father the responsibility of securing human milk to the child through a wet nurse, in cases when the biological mother was unable to provide it. The wet nurse was privileged with a good salary and a status and prerogatives of a family member, in order to ensure that the infant would not be neglected and in order to secure its survival and nourishment (Kocturk, 2003).

4. CRC Principle of a Child's Right to Develop to the Fullest and the Principle of Devotion to the Best Interest of the Child

Proofs of this principle in Islam are many. First, there is the well-known *Hadith* of the Prophet Muhammad (*Peace be upon him*) which states, "Teach your children swimming, archery, and horsemanship." Second, there is the first verse of *surat Al-alaq* (*Al-alaq* chapter) of the Holy Quran which emphasizes God's blessing of teaching man to read and write by the pen. Both of these are examples of the significance Islam gives to the education and development of an individual, not only mentally or intellectually but also physically. Third, before Islam, men were not responsible for their wives or for their offspring. With Islam, however and with women not being allowed more than one spouse, paternity was no longer uncertain and this made men more interested in their own children. They also became more careful about their personal property, with the aim of wanting their offspring to inherit their wealth (Armstrong, 2006). This, certainly, was a very good step towards helping children realize their right of developing to the fullest. Another good step in the same direction was the granting of the women the right to own property, to inherit, and to administer their own wealth, something which was very rare and unheard of in the pre-Islamic period (Armstrong, 2006). By granting women such rights, it became possible for them, if they had children of their own, to offer their sons and daughters a good decent life, with whatever personal property and financial resources they owned. This, in a way, proves that Islam asserts the right of human beings to be given the resources needed for their own development, whether they happen to be men or women or children. Even the institution of polygamy, which has been criticized way too many times as a source of significant suffering to Muslim women, was originally intended to assist in the realization of this particular right. For its main purpose was " ...to correct the injustices done to widows, orphans, and other female dependents, who were especially vulnerable," and who were usually either sold into slavery or forced into prostitution or left with nothing because of a few unscrupulous individuals in the family who seized everything (Armstrong, 2006: 147). The purpose of polygamy, therefore, was for ensuring that unprotected women would be decently married, protected, and taken care of along with their children, if they happened to have any of their own. Polygamy was not designed to gratify the male sexual appetite as is sometimes, unfortunately, believed and practiced but rather it was designed to bring about social justice. Polygamy's real aim, thus, is to help in gratifying a number of women's and children's (especially orphans') essential needs, mainly:

- the need for protection from harm, abuse, and exploitation,
- the need to participate as any other human being in family, cultural, and social life, and
- the need for opportunities to develop to the fullest.

Another highly criticized Islamic practice, which is also central to Judaism, is circumcision of male children. Such a practice has often been attacked as being an act of violence and a form of child abuse. Simply stated, circumcision cannot be considered as abuse because it does not cause injury (Freeman, 1999). What critics of this practice seem to fail to see is that denying a Muslim or Jewish child circumcision would conflict with what is known as the welfare principle, i.e. *what is in the best interests of the child* and, therefore, would conflict with one of the main CRC principles of devotion to a child's interest. For "what is in a child's best interests is to some extent conditioned by the context, which includes the religious context" (Freeman, 1999; 75). In this case, what is in the best interests of a Muslim child- in addition to his protection from catching as a future adult different types of infections, sexually transmitted diseases, and even cancer- is the possession of a cultural identity and the sense of belonging to a certain religious group, both of which compose fundamental human rights. Besides, the relative and temporary harm of the practice of circumcision (i.e., the pain felt at the time of treatment and which the child will usually never remember), in comparison to its short-term and long-term cultural and medical benefits, cannot act as a sufficient condition to deny a child what would constitute his religious and cultural heritage and identity. Muslims, therefore, by insisting on male circumcision, have already been acting in conformity with the principles of CRC even before the CRC itself existed.

Islam, as a result, with (1) the rights it granted women in terms of property ownership and inheritance, (2) the spirit it spread through the certainty of paternity, (3) the protection and security it provided through the institutions of marriage and polygamy, and (4) its insistence on sustaining cultural and religious identity, was from the beginning taking into account first and foremost the best interest of the vulnerable individuals in society, mainly the women and children. Considering this, it is safe to conclude first that all of the guiding principles of CRC happen to be already at the heart of Islam, and second, the rights the CRC grants to children are already rights asserted by Islam as an ideology and ones that are automatically realized with the prevalence of a culture founded on Islam's authentic teachings and practices.

Still, appreciating the dominance and power of religion on the Arab individual, although crucial, is not enough. For what is more important is its utilization for the betterment of the community (*ummah*) and for the purification of society from its ruthless ails- ails such as child abuse and maltreatment in all their forms, including a very often overlooked form discussed in the subsequent chapter, known as *parental alienation*.

Chapter Five

Parental Alienation

Seven-year old Majed stood all alone before the religious judge or 'Shaikh' in a court of law that supposedly abides by the Islamic Shari'ah. He was totally confused about why he was there and felt extremely uncomfortable and somewhat scared of being in such an environment so unfamiliar to him. The judge's attempts to ease his fears and anxieties were totally futile. Nothing worked, not even the small talk about his schoolwork and grades nor about his favorite computer games or friends. What added to his feeling of uneasiness was the fact that no one else was there in the room with him except for a security guard standing right behind the judge. The guard's presence served the primary purpose of protecting the judge from possible conflicts that may on occasion arise between the defendants and the plaintiffs. This specific purpose, though, was not what had been communicated to Little Majed; for he was totally misinformed and told by no one other than his own father that the guard was there to throw him in prison if he chose living with his mother over living with him. His father had made a great effort for two whole weeks prior to this day in court to instill this false belief in his head and he had succeeded. For as soon as the judge asked the little innocent boy the decisive question of whom he wanted to live with, he immediately said: ``I want to live with my father but I love my mother.`` The judge at that point did not even bother to take the time to ask Majed why he wanted to live with his father rather than with his mother, nor to check whether he had been influenced by anyone or anything in his choice. How could he ask such questions when he still had four more cases scheduled for that day? The little boy's answer therefore appeared sufficient for him to issue a *verdict in this custody case and to do so consistently with Islamic law, according to which a boy seven years of age or older should be, all other things considered, granted the parent of his choice to live with. To the judge, it didn't matter at all at that point under what conditions the little boy made his choice nor whether that choice was in his best interests. A choice was made and that was all that counted in deciding the young boy's destiny for the remaining years of his childhood and early adulthood... If only the judge knew what type of life was awaiting poor Little Majed!*

Unfortunately, it was not only Majed who was being affected by the final verdict of this case; it was also his elder sister Maryam, who was eight and a-half years old then and who should have been present in court that same day but had been intentionally prevented from being there by her father. Maryam was way more outspoken than Majed and in a way, she understood the significance of what was to be said in court on that particular occasion. Besides, she was determined to speak out and to express all that she and Majed were suffering by living with their seriously mentally ill father. Unluckily for her, she was kept confined at home and it just broke her heart that the judge did not ask about her whereabouts nor even check with her father why he had not brought her along to court, especially when he had requested from him in an earlier hearing to bring her with him. Her father, of course, out of fear of what she may reveal and describe, decided to keep her home. To her, and as little as she was, that decision was a blow to her rights, not only as a child but also as a human being, and the only way she knew of expressing that type of violation of rights was by saying with tears filling her eyes: ``What hurts the most is that they did not let me speak and explain what it is that I want, or whom I choose to spend the rest of my life with...``

Based on a true custodial case

Custody and the Best Interests of the Child in Islam

Sadly, Majed's and Maryam's scenario above is not an uncommon one in family courts dealing with divorce and custody cases in the Arab World, especially in highly conservative societies that are mainly paternalistic and that claim to abide by Islamic *Shari'ah*. Again, as repeatedly stressed in this book, the problem is not with the Shari'ah itself but in how it is sometimes implemented, especially since abuses of it do unfortunately happen by certain religious jurists, although God clearly orders Muslims in *An-nisaa* (58) verse to act fairly and justly by saying, *"God doth command you to render back your trusts to whom they are due; and when ye judge between man and man, that ye judge with justice"*. God also orders Muslims to always have before their eyes in divorce disputes what is in the best interests of the child. As Ibn Qudaamah al-Maqdisi, an Islamic scholar of the 12th Century, maintained, "custody is aimed at looking after the child, so it should not be given in a way that will be detrimental to his (her) welfare and his (her) religious commitment" (cited by Stacey, 2010; n.p.)

The best interests of the child is something that has been agreed upon by all Muslim scholars and Islamic juristic schools, although over the centuries there have been some disagreements in their views over child custody or, as it is called in Arabic, *hadana*, which refers to "raising, bringing up, or nursing a child" (Zahraa & Malek, 1998; 156). Custody is only for children who are less than seven years of age for after that age, the right to custody turns into what is known as *wilaya* or *kafala*, i.e. respectively, the right to guardianship or sponsorship. When the child is less than seven years old, the mother is more entitled to custody than the father, unless she remarries. If she remarries and custody becomes an issue, then custody is transferred according to the priority of guardians accepted by the Islamic juristic school that the couple belong to (Al-Ghamidi, 2011). Looking at all the juristic schools, we find that after the mother, priority is given first to the women from the mother's side (i.e. maternal grandmother and aunts) and then usually to the women from the father's side, and then finally to the father himself. "Such is the order of priority for guardians. However, in some cases, custody will be awarded in consideration of the best interest of the child without any consideration to the above system. In this case, the child may stay with his mother even if she gets married, but all this can only be decided by the judge" (Al-Ghamidi, 2011; n.p.). Women relatives are given priority in *hadana* cases because it is believed that a woman normally would be more capable of catering to a child's needs than a man. The father however will always be financially responsible for the child regardless of who has custody and of whether the custodial party is rich or poor. The father is obliged by law to provide for the child everything from accommodation to food and drink, clothing, schooling, and other everyday needs. The amount of the financial support however is determined by the father's circumstances and means, as is evident in the Quranic verse *At-Talaq (7)*, which states: *"Let the man of means spend according to his means: and the man whose resources are restricted, let him spend according to what God has given him. God puts no burden on any person beyond what He has given him. After a difficulty, God will soon grant relief"*. In the case if the father dies or is unable to provide for the child and the child has no inherited property, then "providing for the child becomes first the duty of the paternal grandfather, then other paternal relatives, and finally any other living relatives" (Mahdavi, 2008; n.p.). In order to be eligible for *hadana*, both female and male custodians need to satisfy a number of basic conditions, which are, as explained by Zahraa & Malek (1998) the following: (1) they must enjoy full legal capacity, i.e. they need to have attained puberty and maturity and must also be sane; (2) they need to be trustworthy; (3) they need to be physically able to bring up a child, i.e they should be sufficiently healthy, available, and present in the same location as the child; (4) they should not be a religious threat to the child and for this reason it is preferred that they themselves be Muslims, except in the case of a non-Muslim mother who belongs to a monotheistic religion (i.e. a *kitabiyah*) and who does not negatively influence the child's Islamic faith; (5) they need to reside in an area proximal to the non-custodial parent; and (6) in the case of the mother, she should not remarry, for once she remarries, she will lose custody eligibility for fear that "...she will be busy with her new married life at the expense of her duty as a custodian, and hence this would not be in the best interest of the child" (173).

As has been seen above, when a child is younger than seven years old, priority of custody is given to the mother and to the female relatives. Once the child is seven, however, the opinion of the jurists varies (Zahraa & Malek, 1998), since what is distinctive about this age is that it is the age of discernment; i.e. the age when children have the ability to make a choice with respect to which of the two parents they would prefer to stay. Their choice however is dictated by certain conditions (Stacey, 2010), namely that the one they choose will not be someone incapable of protecting and safeguarding them nor one who would forbid them from seeing the other parent (Al-Ghamidi, 2004). According to the Shafi'i juristic school, both male and female children have a right to make such a decision once they are old enough. The case, however, is different for the Hanbali jurists who give this right only to the male child and dictate that a female child should remain with her father until she gets married, unless there are specific circumstances that mandate that she be better off staying with her mother. They argue that a girl is better off with her father, since he is more capable of protecting her from harm and as a guardian, "...he has the capacity to supervise (her) marriage and other aspects of her life..." (Zahraa & Malek, 1998; 168). With respect to the Hanafi and Maliki schools, they both do not agree with such a right of choice. They both argue that a female child is better off staying with the mother until she gets married. As for the male child, the Hanafis believe that once he achieves a certain degree of independence, he is better off with the father; while, the Malikis argue that he should be with the mother until he attains puberty (Zahraa & Malek, 1998; Al-Ghamidi, 2011). In the case of the Ja'afaris, the mother has the custody of the male child until he is seven years old, after which he is given to the father. As for the female child, she stays with the mother until she reaches puberty and then, at that stage, she gets to choose which parent she wants to live with. These differences between the Islamic juristic schools are reflected in the variations of court verdicts issued in custody and guardianship cases around the Arab World; for the courts usually issue their verdicts based on the juristic school followed by the country or area they are in. Despite these variations, however, we find that- as mentioned earlier in this book- although not all Arab countries apply the entire code of Islamic *Shari'ah*, most of them adopt at least a few aspects of it and, in all of them, family law and what is known as the personal status law are derived from and governed by Islamic *Shari'ah*.

This overall background information on custody and guardianship law in Islam can help the reader grasp better our original scenario of Little Majed and his sister Maryam, as it can also help in clarifying why seven-year old Majed was given the opportunity to choose while eight and a-half year old Maryam was not. The fact that Maryam was forced to stay living with her father indicates that the religious court that issued the verdict most probably followed the Hanbali juristic school or, possibly, some other similar trend of judgment. The issue does not really lie in which juristic school or approach was followed; what matters more is the question of whether Maryam's and Majed's best interests were taken into account. Clearly, they were not; for the judge failed to check whether Majed made his choice independently of any pressures and failed to inquire why Maryam was not brought to court despite his earlier request of her to be present on that day. He also failed to take into consideration the particular conditions that should have dictated Majed's choice and which also had a great impact on his sister's life- primarily the condition of not choosing a parent who is incapable of protecting and safeguarding him and his sister and the condition of not choosing someone who would (*as it became obviously clear later on in this particular case*) forbid them from seeing their loving mother.

Parental Alienation as Emotional Abuse

When this last condition is not met and the custodial parent succeeds in forbidding the child from seeing their other parent, this acts as the first sip of what psychologist Dr. Richard Warshak (2003) calls *divorce poison,* in reference to the most under-recognized form of emotional abuse toward children, commonly known as *parental alienation (PA).* Although there is no single accepted definition of alienation (Drozd & Olesen, 2004), PA is "one specific form of post-divorce conflict (that) has been relatively overlooked in the empirical divorce literature...(and it happens)... when one parent turns the child against the other parent through powerful emotional manipulation techniques designed to bind the child to them at the exclusion of the other parent" (Baker, 2005; 289). It can be carried out directly or indirectly; an example of direct PA is when a parent makes a derogatory remark about the other parent or openly blames the other parent for let's say financial difficulties. While, an example of indirect PA is when a parent accepts the negative comments and behaviors of the child towards the other parent. It is important here not to confuse alienating parenting behaviors with protective parenting behaviors; for the latter usually involve appropriate protection and distancing of the child from, for example, an abusive parent (Drozd & Olesen, 2004); while the former, is a form of emotional abuse that involves programming a child in such a way that may not only lead to lifelong alienation of the child from a loving parent but also to lifelong psychological problems in the child (Gardner, 2002). Warshak explains, in one of his interviews on alienation with Maclean's magazine in the June 16 issue of 2008, that "What happens is parents who do this are so caught up in their emotions that they lose sight of their children's needs. They don't deliberately intend to hurt their children" (MacQueen, 2008; 12).

Going back to Majed's and Maryam's scenario, therefore, a recurrent story is usually this: first, the children are given to the parent who won the custody case, *most often the father.* Then, this custodial parent- commonly known in the literature as the *aligning parent*- begins launching an alienating campaign against the target parent, i.e. the parent who eventually may get totally rejected and even hated by the child. The aligning parent is defined as the one who "...systematically influences a child to view the target parent as evil, dangerous, and undesirable in the child's life" (Drozd & Olesen, 2004; 67) until the child begins hating and rejecting that parent. According to Gardner (1998), PA can happen at one of three levels: mild, moderate, and severe, which are explained by Baker (2005; 290) as follows:

> In mild cases there is some parental programming against the other parent but visitation is not seriously affected and the child manages to negotiate having a relationship with both parents without too much difficulty. In cases of moderate parental alienation there is considerable programming against the other parent, resulting in struggles around visitation. The child often has difficulty during the transition from one parent to the other but eventually is able to have a reasonably healthy relationship with both. The child in severe alienation is adamant about his or her hatred of the targeted parent. The child usually refuses any contact and may threaten to run away if forced to visit. The alienating parent and the child have an unhealthy alliance based on shared distorted beliefs about the other parent. The relationship between the child and the targeted parent is completely destroyed.

The reason why PA strategies are considered as forms of child maltreatment is because they usually result in negative feelings in children, like feeling "worthless, flawed, unloved, unwanted, (and) endangered..." (Baker & Ben-Ami, 2011; 473). These feelings develop as a result of the types of things the alienating parent tells the child about the other parent- constantly negative things that always include the message that "...the targeted parent is unsafe, unloving, and unavailable". What reinforces this message is usually the fact that the alienating parent resorts to strategies that limit "...the opportunities for the targeted parent to counter the message, creating the appearance that the targeted parent has rejected the child..." (Baker & Ben-Ami, 2011; 474). In some cases, as explained by Warshak (cited by MacQueen, 2008), the targeted parent contributes to being victimized in this way by "...maintaining a stoic silence or just by refusing to indulge in a similar sort of slander about their ex-spouse" (p.12). Baker and Ben-Ami (2011) maintain that this type of behavior of *taking the high road* might not always be sufficient to counter the negative messages the child is receiving. Warshak adds that "it's not always a good idea to remain passive. Doing nothing leaves the child with no help or understanding of what is at best a confusing situation. In any other situation when children misperceive reality, we help correct their distortions" (p.12). The reason why PA results in a misperceived realty in children is due to the types of alienating strategies that the aligning parents use, like: putting the target parent's love for the child in question; exaggerating the target parent's past mistakes; manufacturing entire episodes to make the target parent look bad; wiping out the child's memories of the good things that were done, in order to not let the child remember that the target parent was present at an important event; and withholding attempts made by the target parent to reach the child, like gifts and cards (Warshak as cited by MacQueen, 2008). Helping correct children's distorted ideas is only one approach for reducing the negative impact that the alienating strategies could possibly have on a child; another, as suggested by Baker and Ben-Ami (2011) is to try to supply the child with the necessary tools, resources, and skills needed to help resist the influences of the alienating strategies and to detect the alienation dynamics they are being subjected to. Of course, not all parents involved in divorce conflicts possess the knowhow of supplying their children with such tools and they are, therefore, in need of some sort of professional training that focuses on psycho-educational prevention approaches.

Another reason why PA is considered psychological maltreatment is because both share the same foundation, basically "...lack of empathy and inability to tolerate the child's separate needs and perceptions" (Baker & Ben-Ami, 2011; 473) and both usually always result in negative outcomes that persist in adulthood. Research findings have long established that parental conflict can determine the long-term adjustment of children of divorce; however, what is more important than the conflict itself is the extent to which the children are drawn into the parental conflict. For "children caught in the middle of parental disputes post-divorce have more problems adjusting than children of divorce who are not thus involved" (Ben-Ami & Baker, 2012; 170). With PA, children are drawn into the parental conflict to a large extent and, as a result, usually develop a higher tendency to suffer from: low self-esteem, self-hatred, depression, lack of trust, identity difficulties, anger, low achievement, substance abuse, divorce, and alienation from their own children (Baker, 2007). O'Sullivan (2012) explains that "the impact of alienation on the child is well documented in the empirical literature. The inner self of the child may disappear as the child is brought up to fulfill the needs of the aligning parent. This may result in the child sacrificing their authentic desires, needs, and characteristics" (p.15).

Parental Alienation in the Muslim Arab World

Going back to our scenario, in several Arab countries, what increases the chances of success of the alienating campaign launched by the custodial parent, is usually the factor of time. For it is often the case that during a custody trial, nothing at all is mentioned about visitation rights nor about financial support for the children nor anything else. Visitation claims and financial dues (*nafaqa*) are considered as separate legal cases, which have to be filed against the parent after the custody case is decided on.

Usually, the time lapse between the custody verdict and the trial for deciding on the visitation rights can be considerably long. It could range from a minimum of three weeks to a maximum of two or even three months, during which the alienating parent, in cases of severe PA, does everything possible to totally cut off the ties between the targeted parent and the child. This timeframe may not seem long in number of days but for the targeted parents, it feels like years because of the suffering they experience for not being able to see their children; at the same time, this time period is usually more than sufficient to start creating in children a state of confusion, and to raise their doubts and suspicions, about the intentions and love of the targeted parents. In other words, it is the time when the seeds of hatred are usually first implanted in the child. This time lapse therefore is of crucial importance, since it usually works strongly against the targeted parent and serves as a winning card in the hands of the alienating parent. Unfortunately, there are absolutely no known empirical studies in the Arab World that address PA in general, nor the impact of this time factor in particular; although, PA cases are clearly abundant and visible in different social groups, socioeconomic classes, communities, and societies. Astonishingly, PA is even visible after the targeted parents gain their visitation rights through a court verdict. For it is often the case that the custodial parent tries to avoid abiding by the court order by not sticking to the visitation schedule and in many cases, unfortunately, gets away with it, either because of what continue to be relatively lax legal systems or by means of some connection (commonly known in Arabic as *wass'ta*) that they may have in the courts or in the law enforcement agencies or the government. This is particularly true when the custodial parent is the father and when he is a man of influence and power. Arab societies, remaining to be mainly paternalistic, make it easier for the man to get away with almost anything and this is probably why we tend to hear of more fathers than mothers being the alienating parents. This contrasts sharply with the results of studies conducted in the United States by Gardner between the early 1980s and mid-1990s, which identified more women than men as the primary alienators (Gardner, 2002). After that time period, though, the number of male alienators started to increase to the point that around 2002, the ratio of male to female alienators became 50/50 and parental alienation became no longer gender specific, as many psychologists have confirmed. Gardner explained this shift by relating it to the fact that after the mid-1990s, men became "...more likely to be primary caretakers, have greater access to the children, and so... (started having)... more time and opportunity to program them" (Gardner, 2002; 105).

Parental Alienation and Mental Illness

Regardless of who is doing the alienation, whether man or woman, the alienator while purposefully intending to hurt the ex-spouse is in reality unintentionally hurting and destroying the child between them. The child is the primary victim and the case becomes extremely grave especially when, as Caddy (2013) explains, "the alienating parent is substantially pathological, where hatred of the other parent is comorbid with quasi-psychotic thinking, or where a shared delusional disorder exists..." (p.362). The most applicable subtype of delusional disorder associated with parental alienation is the persecutory type in which the alienating parent experiences delusions that they are being malevolently treated in some way by the targeted parent (Gardner, 2009). This is exactly what took place in the case of Little Majed and his sister Maryam, who were left to live with a mentally ill father, whose instinctive love for them did not prevent him from cutting them off totally from their mother and her family nor from psychologically and even physically abusing them because of injurious delusions in his head.

In societies where the attitudes towards mental health disorders and illness are in general still strongly linked with cultural variables, such as: reluctance to disclose private information about oneself and family; concerns with personal dignity and prestige; and beliefs in spiritual possessions and the impact of sorcery or the evil eye and the powers of the religious traditional healer or *Shaikh*, as he is commonly called (Okasha et al, 2012); the situation for Arab children (like Majed and Maryam) living with parents who suffer from some form of mental illness is therefore almost hopeless. What complicates things even more is the stigma and considerable degree of ignorance surrounding mental illness in the Arab World (Adams, 2011). For example, mental disorders are usually simply identified with "craziness"; many people do not know that there are different types of disorders and different levels of severity (Adams, 2011); sometimes, mental illness is considered as a punishment from God and mentally ill individuals are seen as mentally retarded or possessed by evil spirits or as dangerous or even something to be ashamed of and avoided (Bener & Ghuloum, 2011). Misconceptions like these pose serious challenges for mental health practitioners in the Arab Region, for such false beliefs make it more difficult for them to benefit their patients or to even just be accepted and approached by those who are actually in need of their services. This is especially true since people's first choice, in general, is to go, or to take someone, to the religious traditional healer or *Shaikh* when experiencing emotional or mental problems rather than seeking the professional help of a mental health practitioner; unfortunately, many times these *Shaikh*s are not really *Shaikh*s and are just in it for the money (Adams, 2011). It is important to note here that mental health practice as we know it today is in no way inconsistent with Islamic teachings. It is true that the words and verses of the Quran are considered by Muslims as possessing a healing power for humankind's woes and ills but "it is equally important to understand that it is permissible and at times obligatory, to seek help from medical practitioners" (Stacey, 2008; n.p.) "According to the Prophet Muhammad, 'God has created a cure for every illness except death.' Thus, Muslims are commanded, as both scientist and patient, to 'seek the cure.' The heritage of Islamic medical history and the prominence of Muslim medical researchers today indicate a generally pro-medical science attitude among most Muslims" (Boston University School of Medicine Website, 2012; n.p.).

Another cultural factor that commonly acts as a barrier in the face of positive mental health treatment outcomes, especially in highly paternalistic Arab societies, is "the tendency for Arab men to underreport their experience of psychiatric symptoms and disorders, which is probably related to their perceived stigmatizing impact and exposing men's vulnerability when they are expected to be resilient and always in control" (Tanios et al, 2009; 417). With such negative attitudes, cultural beliefs, and misbeliefs, there is a slight chance- if any- that a parent suffering from a mental illness is going to seek the help of a mental health practitioner. There is also a slight chance that one of their parents or siblings will try to seek such professional help for them on their behalf, out of protection of their family name, image, social status, or prestige. As Psychiatrist Ziad Kronfol explains in one of his interviews with *Nature Middle East* in July 2012, with the absence in the Arab World of mental health acts and policies that (1) balance the rights of the mentally ill for safety and quality care with their rights for freedom and confidentiality and (2) govern different scenarios involving the mentally ill and when they should be forced into treatment to protect them or others from possible adverse consequences of their illness; the mentally ill can still suffer from different forms of abuse or neglect (Yahia, 2012). What increases the possibility of neglecting to seek professional help for the mentally ill is the fact that in most Arab countries, mental health is not yet financially covered or insured- like other medical disorders are- and can therefore be costly for the less advantaged classes of society. Those looking after a mentally ill individual may therefore opt for ignoring their illness or learning to live with it rather than paying for their treatment.

On a more positive note and despite all of this, significant changes have taken place in the field of mental health in the Arab Region in recent years; for example, there has been an increase in psychiatric services (Okasha, 2012), some countries have been trying to incorporate mental health services into their primary health-care systems (Adams, 2011), and there has been an increase in awareness of the importance of mental health problems and their treatment, although such awareness needs yet to be translated into action (Yahia, 2012) and needs to be coupled with a change in cultural beliefs surrounding psychiatry and psychotherapy (Bener & Ghuloum, 2011). Still however such positive changes are important and necessary, just as investments in factors characteristic to the Arab region like strong family ties and religion are. For, as Psychiatrist Ziad Kronfol explains, family ties in the Arab World can play a positive role in mental health practice, since they can be "used as social support rather than social pressure"; while religion "could be positive to the extent that it induces good deeds and protects the person from harm, including self-inflicted harm" (Yahia, 2012; n.p.). Such investments and positive changes are crucial in a region of the world that in general has been for decades- and unfortunately continues to be- a stage for political instability, military conflicts and wars, violence, and unfavorable and stressful economic conditions. For, the latter are all factors that usually result in at-risk groups that are specifically vulnerable to mental illnesses- particularly post-traumatic stress disorder (PTSD)- like war survivors, displaced individuals, refugees, exploited workers, etc. (Yahia, 2012). In addition to PTSD, other common illnesses prevalent are anxiety disorders like social phobia, schizophrenia and delusional disorders, depressive disorders, as well as a high rate of comorbidity. The Arab World, therefore, does not differ much from the rest of the world in terms of types of mental health problems as well as in frequency; at least, this is what the few statistics coming out of some Arab countries (like Lebanon, Egypt, Iraq, and Morocco) confirm (Yahia, 2012).

Mental health problems, therefore, are a fact in the Arab societies and if political instability, turmoil, and economic problems continue to exist, it is safe to expect rates of mental illness and character disorders to be on the rise. With this, forms of child abuse will at least persist if not prevail even more, since as mentioned in chapter three of this book one of the main causes of child abuse is the high rates of mental disorders. Parental alienation, as a kind of emotional abuse, is therefore also expected to have the same fate, and when practiced by a parent with mental illness, the situation for the child becomes critical and sadly, in some cases, life-threatening, depending on the severity of the mental illness the parent is suffering from and the degree of isolation the parent is enforcing on the child. In our case of Majed and Maryam, their father suffering from a delusional paranoid disorder, cut them off totally from all their family members and friends. Even direct family members from his side were to him suspicious and considered in many cases as conspiring against him and even trying to harm him. The mother, in particular, was seen as the master planner of his persecution and so he did everything in his power to portray her to Majed and Maryam as the devil in disguise, whom they should avoid so as to not get harmed by her the same way she has been trying to harm him. To help convince them of the need to avoid her, he made sure to remove all their photos with her from the house that could remind them of the good times they had with her; he banned them to answer or use the telephone, in case she tried to call them or they felt like calling her; he rehearsed with them calling her bad names and describing her with the most appalling adjectives he knew; and he even threatened to burn her or kill her, if she tried coming near their house, and simultaneously told the children that she was not trying to come visit them because she did not want to see them- *all of which happen to clearly be actions taken to alienate the mother from the children.*

Factors Impacting Parental Alienation Attempts

Despite, the father's forceful alienation attempts, however, he was not successful at making Majed and Maryam hate their mother or begin to reject her. Consistently with this, research studies have shown that alienation attempts do not always succeed because it all depends on: (1) the strength of the attachment bond that was established before the divorce between the non-custodial parent and the child; (2) the age of the child; and (3) the child's level of emotional intelligence and capacity to analyse and think critically, which can help them not accept everything they are told without discrimination. Bone & Walsh (1999) explain that the younger a child is, the more vulnerable they are to alienation strategies and tend to take unfavourable messages directed against the non-custodial parent uncritically. Another factor that may impact the success chances of parental alienation is the parental tenacity of the target parent; the more the target parent is willing to stick around and not to give up, the weaker are the chances that parental alienation attempts will succeed. Bone & Walsh (1999) also add that the phenomenon of when the child is not successfully alienated but nevertheless the criteria of parental alienation are present is known as "attempted" parental alienation, which they argue is "still quite harmful and the fact of children not being alienated should not be viewed as neutral by the court. Any attempt at alienating the children from the other parent should be seen as a direct and wilful violation of one of the prime duties of parenthood" (p.44). Unfortunately, not yielding to the alienating parent's wishes and defying them, especially by expressing positive approval of the absent parent, usually results in a high price to pay on the part of the child. For, the relationship in alienation is one based on fear: the custodial parent is afraid of the child abandoning them and going to the distant parent and the child, on his part, is afraid of retaliation from the custodial parent, who constantly threatens to abandon them and to reject them and does this openly and vehemently, particularly when the child disobeys their alienating directives. "Children under these conditions live in a state of chronic upset and threat of reprisal (and)...develop an acute sense of vigilance over displeasing the alienating parent" (Bone & Walsh, 1999; 47).

In the case of Majed and Maryam, their father's unsuccessful alienation attempts only aggravated things for them. Since, these failed attempts did not only increase their father's already existing fear of abandonment- which is a characteristic symptom of all alienating parents (Childress, 2013)- but they also led him to treat poor Majed and Maryam themselves as part of the conspiracy to harm him, because of some mysterious powers the mother had that enabled her to bring them in on her persecutory plot and plan. They, as a result, frequently got severely punished (*abused*) for deeds that they did not really do but were only the result of delusions in their father's head because of his delusional paranoid disorder. The problem is that with the absence of their mother, other relatives, and friends, they were despondently left alone to deal with their father's illness with no protection whatsoever.

In cases like these, all symptoms of the parent's mental illness get cast on the defenceless child, who is already suffering from the harmful effects of *attempted* PA they are being subjected to. The child therefore is being doubly maltreated here by being a victim first of *attempted* PA and secondly of abuse resulting from the parent's mental condition.

Unfortunately, Majed and Maryam are not alone in such type of suffering; there are many children like them especially children belonging to single-parent families, in which as indicated by research studies child abuse tends to be more common than in two-parent families (Ibrahim et al, 2008). This is particularly true in single-parent families where psychiatric problems are present or where a third party (*e.g. a stepmother or a stepfather or a fiancé or even a housemaid etc.*) is given the chance to participate in the abuse of the child. The subsequent chapter presents a brief but painful review of prominent and appalling child abuse cases from several Arab countries, which had gone public over the past five to six years and which also took place in households with only one biological parent and, in some cases, with a third party present. The main objective of presenting these cases is to show how *haste* or *injudicious* or *uncorroborated* or even *biased* verdicts in what are supposedly Islamic family courts- when it comes to who gains custody of a helpless child- may sentence a child to torture in a worldly hell spelled H.O.M.E...

Chapter Six

As they had for me?

"Thy Lord hath decreed that ye worship none but Him, and that ye be kind to parents. Whether one or both of them attain old age in thy life, say not to them a word of contempt, nor repel them, but address them in terms of honor. And, out of kindness, lower to them the wing of humility, and say: "My Lord! Bestow on them thy Mercy even as they cherished me in childhood" (Al-isra'a, 23, 24).

The Quranic verses *Al-isra'a (23) and (24)* stated above are two of the most recited verses in everyday discourses in the Arab World, due to the high standing they attribute to parents and to the guidance they present to sons and daughters, with respect to how they should treat their parents, especially in their old age. Looking closely at *verse 24*, and precisely at the second part of it which in reference to parents states, "as they cherished me in childhood" (or sometimes translated "as they cared for me in childhood" or "merciful as they brought me up when little"), one easily notices what can be considered as a truism. It is a truism not just from anyone, but from God Himself about how parents naturally treat their youngsters, *mainly as cherished beings worthy of mercy and care*. Anything contrary to such treatment, therefore, is a deviation from what is natural and from what is considered by God as the way things are. This verse also seems to carry a hidden and indirect conditional statement for parents, as a reminder that if they want their sons and daughters to pray for them not only in their old age but also after their death- which is something of *extreme* importance to Muslims-, they need to abide by the natural merciful ways of bringing up their children. This is in line with the Prophet's Hadith (*Peace be upon him*): "Whoever is not merciful to others will not be treated mercifully." (Al-Bukhari cited by Amatullah Abdullah, 2014; n.p.)

Cases Disobedient to Allah's Decree

Reading or listening to the news from different parts of the Arab World, however, makes one realize the big number of cases in which parents seem to tend to forget or ignore this condition indirectly implied by *verse 24* of *Al-isra'a*. The end result, as a consequence, usually is some form of child abuse, mostly physical and sometimes a combination of physical, emotional, and even sexual abuse. What is noticeable about the majority of the cases reported is that they are cases that took place in single-parent families where the other parent was distant and, in some instances, a stepmother or a stepfather was present. What follows is a description of some of these cases that represent clear examples of parents who completely turned a blind eye to the conditional message of *Al-isra'a* (24).

In the year 2008, there was the story reported by the Saudi *Al-Watan Newspaper* of a father brutally beating his daughter with a piece of wood, which subsequently resulted in her death, and all because the girl had tried to get in touch with her mother whom he had divorced. In the same year, there was also in Tabuk-Saudi Arabia, the famous story of five-year-old *Bayan*, whose mother was estranged, and who was brutally beaten to death by her custodial father after she consistently refused to obey him. While in Yemen, the devastating story of sixteen-year old *Berdees* was discovered after the girl had been imprisoned by her father and stepmother in a room for eight whole years. The same year, in Amman, Jordan, a 49-year-old man was arrested for having molested and raped his then 17-year-old daughter since she was nine. In addition to the sexual abuse, he had often physically assaulted her in order to discipline her, as he later confessed in court. He also had constantly threatened to kill her if she ever exposed him to anyone. At the age of thirteen, the girl had become pregnant as a result of the rapes and delivered a baby boy. The court transcripts stated that the father had divorced his wife when his daughter was only six months old and she was then taken to her aunt's house to be looked after. At the age of nine, she was sent to live with her father, where an older brother of hers was already living. The nine-year-old girl was sleeping with the father in the same room while her brother slept in a second room of the house. On October 3rd, 2008, the girl found enough courage to finally inform her brother and one of her cousins of her father's crimes and they went and filed a case against him in the Family Protection Department. The father was immediately arrested and then finally sentenced to death in 2012, according to the October 2nd, 2012 news report of Rana Husseini for the *Jordan Times* news website.

Many similar other cases were also reported in 2009 and most of them were child abuse cases that resulted in the death of the child and that were committed by the child's father and stepmother, with the biological mother being divorced and estranged. The most famous is that of the nine-year-old *Areej*, who was tortured to death by not only being beaten, but by also having a hot iron pressed on different parts of her little body. As was reported by the Saudi *Arab News* newspaper, her deceased body was discovered by the Red Crescent Society thrown outside her home. In 2010, as was reported by the Emirati *Gulfnews*, a seven-year-old boy from Ajman, United Arab Emirates was found with severe bruises, black eyes, and marks indicating that he had been hit on the head, back, hands, face, and other parts of his body as a result of being repeatedly beaten by his father and stepmother. The year before that, a nine-year-old girl in Abu-Dhabi, United Arab Emirates was rushed to the hospital bleeding and with burns, knife cuts, and bruises on her body after having been tortured by her father and stepmother.

In 2011, the horrific story of the torture and murder of five-year-old *Lama* and her father's monstrosity in Saudi Arabia went public on a number of news websites and television channels. When *Lama* was taken to hospital, she had a crushed skull, broken left arm and ribs, a torn fingernail, and a torn rectum. This was clearly a case of both physical and sexual abuse and again in this case *Lama's* mother was divorced from the father and estranged. In March 2012 and in the old port town of Larache, Morocco, the news of the death of 16-year-old *Amina Filali* aroused outrage around the world. *Amina* had been raped at the age of 15 and was then forced by her parents and a judge to marry her rapist, in order to protect the family honor. After about six months of marriage, during which she suffered recurrent beatings, she committed suicide by ingesting rat poison. Amina's death flared up many protests in the country which eventually led the parliament to abolish a previous penal code that allowed rapists to escape prosecution if they married their underage victims. In this case, Amina had undergone double tragedy first by getting raped and then by being forced to get married to her rapist. Although the first abuse was committed by the rapist, probably the more serious breach of her rights was done by no other than her parents and the judge when they forced her into the ruthless marriage.

In April 2012 and in Al-Minya governate of Egypt, as was reported by *Al Youm Al Sabea'a* newspaper, a father killed his three young daughters aged seven, five, and three by buying two cobra snakes and letting them bite the girls while sleeping in their beds at night. The father had earlier divorced the girls' mother because he doubted her and alleged that she had been in a relationship with another man. While in June 2012, in the United Arab Emirates, there was the shocking story of eight-year old *Wadima* who was tortured and beaten to death by her father and his girlfriend and whose little body was afterwards buried in the desert. The two had used iron rods and boiling water to burn both *Wadima* and her seven-year old sister *Meyra* with for a period of six whole months. The crime was discovered only after *Meyra*, who was left with 10% permanent disability, informed a relative of the sixth-months ordeal she and her sister had been through. In 2012 also, the appalling story of *Hanan* from Al-Madinah, in Saudi Arabia made the news headlines. Sixteen years earlier, Hanan had been nine-years old when her father tied her up in the main hall of their house and beat her to death while her stepmother and her children watched. He then took her body and secretly buried it in a remote area outside the city and afterwards rushed his family to the neighbouring holy city of Makkah, claiming to want to visit *Al-Masjid Al-Haram*- Islam's most sacred mosque there. When in Makkah, he filed a report at the nearest police station claiming that his nine-year-old daughter had gone missing among the crowds at the mosque. Hanan's body was accidentally discovered that same year due to heavy rains that hit Al-Madinah and exposed her grave; however, since no one was able to identify the body, she was placed in the morgue for some time and then buried by the authorities. In 2012, sixteen years later, *Hanan's* stepmother came forward and informed the police of her husband's crime and, as a result, the curiosity of *Hanan's* estranged mother, who had been searching for her daughter for 16 years, bitterly came to an end.

These are just a few examples of many more abuse cases that have made it on the news in the Arab Gulf region and in Arab countries elsewhere. What is certain is that such cases- like other medically reported ones- "are the most severe ones ...and these children are most likely to represent just the tip of the iceberg while most of the less severe cases go unnoticed and unreported" (Al-Mahroos, 2007; 245). These cases are also consistent with research findings that have indicated that child abuse is more common in single-parent families and also where psychiatric problems are present (Ibrahim et al, 2008).

Why More Female Victims?

What is especially noticeable about these cases and others like them that made the news, is that the majority of them involved female victims rather than males. This could be due to several factors: some demographical, some cultural, and some psychological. Demographically, it could be because the sex ratio in the Arab countries (except for Somalia) for females and males under 15 years of age indicates a greater number of females than males (World DataBank, 2012), and so it is natural to have more female abuse cases than males. Culturally, it could be because a lot of Arab families still value sons more than daughters because of the son being the perpetuator of the family name. Girls are therefore sometimes looked down upon, while boys are treated with more care and regard in the context of some families, which may explain why we hear of more abuse cases involving females than males. Finally, with respect to the psychological factor, there is a higher chance that girls resemble their mothers more than the boys and since most of the abusive parents in the stories we hear about are single fathers, then it could be that a father, by having unresolved feelings of anger or retaliation towards his ex-wife, tends to take out such negative emotions on his daughter because of her resemblance to her mother. In psychological terms, this mechanism is known as *displacement*, and tends to happen often in high-conflict families, especially when the custodial parent is unable to express their anger towards the distant parent, either because they are inaccessible or out of fear of negative consequences and, as a result, express it instead towards the defenceless child who poses no threat to them whatsoever. When the child is of the same gender as the distant parent and when the resemblance between them is great, the chances of displacement become higher. The fact that in most of the cases reported above and in many other cases on the news, such displacement is being directed mainly on little girls is both unfortunate and completely un-Islamic; for Islam in no way discriminates between boys and girls in treatment and, actually, orders that both genders be treated equally and considers treating them differently as a sin (Muslim Academy, 2013). The Prophet (*Peace be upon him*) was in fact reported as saying: "Fear Allah and treat your children [small or grown] fairly (with equal justice)" (Al-Bukhari cited by Amatullah Abdullah, 2014; n.p.). He was also reported as saying: "Be fair and just in terms of the gifts you offer your children. If I was to give preference to any (gender over the other) I would have preferred females over males (in terms of giving gifts)" (Al-Sheha, 1997; 33-34). *Hadiths* like these, as well as the Prophet's dealings with- and attitude towards- children, are an example for the whole of humanity of how children are to be treated and cherished at all times, regardless of their gender. Irrespective of the factor, therefore, whether demographical, cultural, or psychological, there is no justification in Islam for mistreating girls over boys, just as there is no validation for mistreating any child or human being or even animal. Nurturing, caring, cherishing, loving, and being merciful are the only justified ways of dealing with God's beings.

Accountability of Judges in Family Courts

To sum up, the painful cases that were presented in this chapter, as well as many others like them not reported here, make one wonder why in the first place the maltreated children ended up with such abusive parents. What is certain is that *the best interest of the child* could not have been taken into consideration in the custody trials of these children, or else, they would have probably ended up with a better fate. The question that imposes itself here therefore is who is to be held accountable for entrusting these children to the wrong hands? As we explained in a previous chapter, Islamic jurisprudence itself with all that it decrees cannot be held responsible with respect to who should gain custody. For, in every particular court hearing, as Al-Ghamidi (2011) explains, custody should be awarded in consideration of the best interest of the child, without necessarily always abiding by the order of priority of the guardians prescribed by the relevant juristic school. It is necessary however to ensure that whoever is awarded the custody is truly worthy of such privilege. As detailed earlier, to be eligible for custody, one must be: physically capable, healthy, and present; mature; sane; trustworthy; and religiously, a positive influence on the child. One must also be available, meaning not too preoccupied to the point of not giving enough attention and time to the child and finally, one must not attempt to alienate the child from their non-custodial parent. It is the responsibility of the judge in court- and his alone- thus to arduously assess the eligibility of a party claiming custody, before issuing any verdict that will impact a child's life forever. Such assessment is to be carried out meticulously through the collection of data and evidence from numerous witnesses and testimonies about the qualification of this party. Above all, it is the judge's responsibility to assess eligibility through the eyes of no one but the child whose custody is at stake, if the child's age of course allows it. The child's assessment of this party, preferences as to whom to live with, and reasons for- or justification of- their preferences, should be among the main determining factors in court hearings such as these, simply because the child is the most impacted party in all this and has a right from God to express their point of view in this matter. In other words, the right of the child to choose is a divine right like all other children's rights. To act in a truly Islamic manner, therefore, the judge should not deny the child this right and should focus on the reasons they give to support their choice; for, the types of reasons expressed are what can provide the judge with a sense of whether the child's choice is totally their own or whether it had been made in advance for them by someone else. Focusing on these reasons and taking as much time as is needed to test their validity is therefore crucial before any final verdict is issued.

No more should judges in family courts then expedite the process of arriving at a decisive outcome, as has usually been happening in the Arab World. No more should they be allowed also to get away with issuing biased and partial verdicts in the interest of one of the two conflicting parents over the main interest of the child, as some of them do. Finally, no more should they be given the opportunity to interpret jurisprudence according to their whim and based on what suits them better. There should be, in brief, absolutely no easy way out for them! Measures therefore are needed to monitor how judges in family courts operate and to hold them accountable for any type of corruption or negligence involved in fulfilling their main responsibilities. A culture change is consequently due, in order to give cases like custody and guardianship precedence in the legal systems. It is also needed in order to raise the awareness of people, in general, and to educate them about the seriousness of such cases and the detrimental consequences possible when the wrong and unwise verdicts are made due to taking matters lightly or to not giving them the time and attention they deserve. Every custody case deals with a life to be offered to a child and thus cases like these are worthy of changes not only on the individual and legal levels but also on the societal and national level as a whole. Congruently, the prevention of child abuse in all shape and form and regardless of where or when or by whom it happens, is worthy of the same changes. The chapter that follows, as a result, attempts to propose a framework that explains the types of measures, cultural changes, and structural modifications needed to be implemented to combat child abuse in the Arab World, with all the religious, cultural, and social specificities of it as a region.

Chapter Seven

A Practical Framework for Protecting Children's Rights In the Muslim Arab World

The tragic cases described in the previous chapter, although originating from born Muslims, are the farthest away from Islam, its principles, and values of mercy and compassion. They are actually a disgrace to the whole Muslim Arab World. They are also manifestations of negligence and lack of awareness about the ominous consequences of child abuse in all its forms, as well as, being indicators of ignorance about proper parenting styles and the correct ways of disciplining and bringing up children. They furthermore are expressions of lack of internal constraint, moral values, and religious righteousness- all of which normally prevent an adult from hurting a child. Last but not least, they are representations of lack of accountability and of what seem to be lax legal systems when it comes to the protection of children, as well as, corrupt judicial systems that deny a child their rights, mainly their right to choose and express the life they want and why they want it.

Despite the fact that several Arab countries have taken a long stride by issuing new laws and ratifying international conventions of children's rights, still attempts at the enforcement of such laws and conventions seems to be in most cases weak, isolated, and fragmented. The proof is simply the big number of child abuse cases continuing to prevail in Arab societies, in all forms and in different contexts, whether at home or at school or among vulnerable displaced and refugee groups or in the streets, etc. Much more is needed therefore in the Arab World, in order to reduce the magnitude of child abuse and other children's rights violations, if not to put a complete end to them. The question though is this: What is it exactly that is needed for tackling a problem from which all countries in the world suffer? This chapter attempts to provide an answer by proposing a practical framework that describes the types of measures, cultural changes, and structural modifications needed to be implemented to address child abuse and violations of children's rights in the Muslim Arab World, while taking into account all the religious, cultural, and social specificities of the region.

Diagram 1 below summarizes the key entities and the relationships between them, as well as their processes, suggested by this framework as the key players involved in protecting children's rights. This framework is grounded in the conviction that each of the Arab countries is in dire need for a social reform at the national level, similar to other types of reforms (e.g. economic or educational etc.) currently taking place in many of them. The aspect of social reform that this framework is concerned with is increased protection for children and the realization of their rights, which should be articulated into an initiative from the government or state, as is the case with any other type of national reform movement. Of course, for any reform to succeed, it requires cultural changes and particularly in this case a change in the mind-set of people with respect to how they view children. People in the Arab countries need to move from seeing children mainly as vulnerable and innocent beings or as incomplete adults to considering them as rights-bearing individuals and as social actors. As explained in an earlier chapter, this latter way of looking at children portrays the child as carrying sacred rights and as individual-rights, that are distinct from the family and the community one lives in, and affirms the child's full human capacities in making decisions about their lives. This outlook is usually most evident in movements that target children's oppression and argue for their voices to be heard. For this reason, it seems to be a very fitting outlook for the type of reform called for by the proposed framework here. What adds to its aptness is the fact that it is in no way inconsistent with Islamic views. Since, as was clarified before, the rights of children in Islam are divine and their opinions and preferences are to be respected and genuinely taken into account at all times.

Framework for Protecting Children's Rights

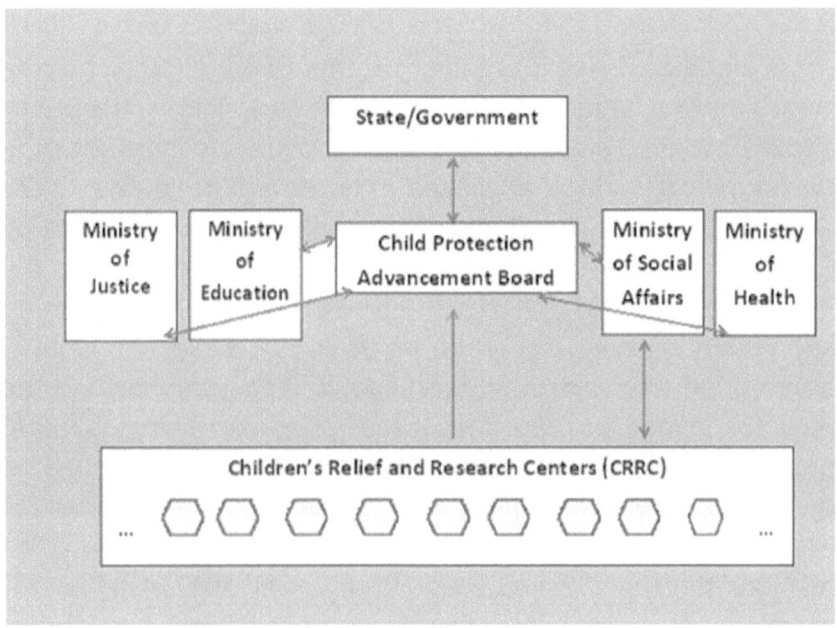

Diagram 1

The social reform initiative from the government should be tied to a specific vision pre-set also by the state and to be pursued by each and every social entity in the nation. This vision should exist independently and not as a subpart of some other overriding vision, so as to stand out and be given the weight and importance it deserves. It should also provide a clear direction for creating and sustaining an enhanced life for children. The heart of this vision should be *a shared goal of providing a safe and healthy society in which children enjoy a dignified life and develop their full potential, through their awareness of, exercise, and realization of their divine rights.* Following the launch and dissemination of its vision, which we propose to call here the *Children's Welfare Vision*, the government needs to establish an executive board possibly known as the *Child Protection and Advancement Board (CPAB)*, to lead the process of setting- with a number of ministries- a roadmap that helps in the achievement of this vision. The ministries involved should mainly be the Ministry of Social Affairs, Ministry of Justice, Ministry of Health, and Ministry of Education- the role of which will be elaborated on later in this chapter.

A significant responsibility of the CPAB should be the launching of a nationwide media campaign to inform the public about *Children's Welfare Vision* and its connectedness with the government's strategic advances. In terms of Kurt Lewin's 1940's *Three-Step Process for Change Model*, this duty to be taken by CPAB is a crucial one falling within the *unfreeze* stage, which is the first of three stages of change. It involves, in addition to defining and communicating the vision or goals- i.e. explaining what is going on and to where the road should lead-, emphasizing the need for change and why it must take place. As Lewin, the father of change management, put it, "Motivation for change must be generated before change can occur. One must be helped to re-examine many cherished assumptions about oneself and one's relations to others." (cited by Bradbury et al, 2007; 81). This re-examining of oneself and of one's relations is similar to what is called for in the Holy Quran through verse *Ar-ra'd* (11): *"Verily never will God change the condition of a people until they change it themselves"*. The resemblance lies in the fact that this verse emphasizes that for change to happen, each person needs to start with themselves, their beliefs, assumptions, relations, and actions. To begin with changing themselves, however, people need a reason to motivate them. The CPAB therefore needs to rely in its media campaign on this Quranic verse, and others similar to it, for its relevance to the Muslim Arab World. It also needs- before asking Arab societies to change their ways of looking at and dealing with children- to first bring to the surface the types of problems existing with respect to child protection and explain the rationale why such problems need to be eradicated. The rationale itself though may not be sufficient to initiate the change, since the unfreezing stage may involve different problems, especially with people who are resistant to change and who are so clenched to their own beliefs and actions, sometimes to a prejudiced degree. The psychologist Gordon Allport explained that in order to remove prejudices, a process of 'catharsis" or *purification from ones emotions, complexes, and feelings* is needed and which can be achieved through a deliberate emotional stir-up (Lewin, 1947). What this implies therefore is that the media campaign of the CPAB should include vivid powerful scenes and stories of child abuse cases and violations of children's rights in all their forms and contexts, in order to stir up the emotions of the public, and make them re-examine their views, attitudes, and actions towards children. The campaign should also accentuate Islamic principles, *Hadith*, and Quranic verses that condemn child maltreatment and that reward merciful mannerisms. The re-examination of self is important because it makes people question their beliefs, to check if they are really well-founded and true or whether they are just mere assumptions. When bringing up children or dealing with them in any way, assumptions are not enough, especially with the complexities of this age and time, the multitude of impacting factors, and the increased demands and needs of youngsters, which require from adults wise decisions, proper child-rearing practices, and treatments that are based on awareness, knowledge, and competence. Assumptions therefore are not sufficient when it comes to children, just as they can never measure up to what is factual or true. Evidence for this is even found in the Quran and in specific in verse *Yunus* (36): *"But most of them follow nothing but fancy (assumptions): truly fancy (assumptions) can be of no avail against truth. Verily God is well aware of all that they do"*.

It is hoped therefore that with the dissemination of the *Children's Welfare Vision* and its connectedness to the government's strategic advances; the emphasis on the need and rationale for change; the deliberate emotional stir-up; the re-examination of self and relations to others; and the questioning of the truthfulness of beliefs; the public will be more ready for accepting the targeted cultural and social change and will thus be ready for stage 2 of Lewin's Change Model- *the moving (transitioning) stage.*

In this second stage, the CPAB needs to start working closely with ministries to assist each of them in forming a steering committee *(a guiding team)* that not only shares the same values and goals of the CPAB but also works on spreading them within its ministry directorates and involving others in their dissemination, in order to achieve personnel *buy-in*. This committee will have at its core the direction of the ministry strategies towards the realization of *Child Welfare Vision* and the management and monitoring of projects that are coherent with established relevant aims. Part of the committee's work is to create working groups of *experts* that will help implement the projects within the ministry. All of the projects should at the first stage aim at preparing and developing the ministry personnel to embrace the new changes and second, reach out to the public to assist with raising their awareness and educating them through programs that focus on children's rights as an issue with all its interrelated facets. Below is a separate description of the types of projects and programs to be implemented by each ministry.

Ministry of Health

Speaking in more detail, the Ministry of Health would have to provide hospital staff all over the country with training programs on how to spot signs of child maltreatment, how to properly document and report it, and how to refer child victims to counseling and rehabilitation. It would also need to find ways to support and assure hospital staff of protection, so that they would not be "reluctant to report suspected cases of abuse and neglect, in order to avoid any complications that might arise in the event that allegations are not substantiated" (Al Eissa & Almuneef, 2010; 32). It would also have to offer the public programs on the adverse physical, psychological, and behavioral effects of child neglect and abuse in all its forms, in addition to programs on the proper ways of nourishing and nurturing children. Finally, it needs to ensure the provision of affordable (or even *free* in the case of the rich countries), sufficient, and high quality mental health services to help child victims not only survive but also thrive after their traumatic abusive experiences and to treat adults dealing with children from their own psychological problems and complexes.

Ministry of Justice

The Ministry of Justice, as explained in an earlier chapter, needs to first establish- through its steering committee- measures that would monitor how judges in courts operate and to hold them accountable for any type of corruption or negligence involved in fulfilling their responsibilities. Some of these measures are (1) the equipping of a team of examiners who are both knowledgeable about Islamic *Shari'ah* and jurisprudence and are children's rights experts, (2) their assignment as monitors in trials involving children to evaluate and report on the performance of judges, and (3) the establishment of penal committees to question the malpractice of judges when necessary. The presence of the examiners in the trials will help ensure that judges fulfill their duties in a more responsible and impartial manner and that children are prevented from possibly being issued verdicts that are against their interests. The Ministry needs to also put together professional development programs that refresh the memories of judges and other ministry personnel with respect to the divine rights of children- as God-given rights- and that educate them about the detrimental consequences possible when the wrong and unwise verdicts are made, due to taking matters lightly or to not giving them the time and attention they deserve. Such programs should rely mainly on the examination and analysis of previous legal cases involving children from all over the world but mainly from the Muslim Arab World, in order to demonstrate how the lives of little children may have been impacted inversely had the issued verdicts been any different. Finally, the Ministry should also work on sponsoring and providing awareness programs that (1) enlighten children about their own rights and about how to ask for them and (2) educate adults who deal with children about children's rights, what counts and what does not count as a violation of those rights, and the legal consequences of any type of violation. In addition, the Ministry needs to coordinate its efforts with the law enforcement agencies (police stations), in order to ensure awareness among police officers of children's rights; signs of child maltreatment; the difference between disciplining a child and abusing a child; and the dirty games some parents play to distort the facts and escape penalty by not complying with some official legal outcome, like granting the other parent their specific visitation right or paying the *nafaqa* (child support) due, etc. The ministry should also double its efforts with the police, in order to guarantee the strict execution of laws protecting children and the infliction of harsh punishments on the transgressors.

Ministry of Social Affairs

The Ministry of Social Affairs *(regardless of its specific name)* in any Arab country is probably the most active entity when it comes to the protection of children. Its services usually include care for children, the elderly, and people with disabilities as well as support for human rights issues and associated non-governmental organizations. Although this ministry in some countries coordinates with other ministries in work related to child protection, the coordination is still deficient, since in many of the ministries, personnel are not yet sufficiently trained nor confident about working with cases of child abuse and neglect, nor are they clear on the priority and sacredness to be attributed to children's rights. For sure, there are those who are enthusiastic about the whole issue but the *buy-in* and preparedness is still not up to the level that is needed nor up to the level that could be reached under a framework similar to the one being proposed in this book. The reason for this is that within this framework, efforts between ministries are to be coordinated by the CPAB under *one shared governmental vision* at which the *whole nation* will be aiming to achieve. In addition, each ministry will be directed by a *well-informed* and *reform-focused* steering committee which will lead and guide working groups of *experts* that will help implement a variety of projects related to protection of children's rights.

According to the proposed framework, the basis of the work to be done by the Ministry of Social Affairs, in addition to all the services it already includes or supervises, is to establish *Child Relief and Research Centers (CRRC)* in the different provinces of the country. Generally, each province should have one center unless it is big in area, then it should have more than one. These centers are to function under the directives of the Ministry of Social Affairs but are to feedback information to all the ministries through the CPAB. Their main responsibilities are similar to currently existing human rights and children protection centers *(e.g. the Child Protection Center in the Kingdom of Bahrain)* in terms of: caring for children exposed to any kind of harm; providing psychological, social and educational services; coordinating legal and judicial services; providing temporary or permanent foster care when necessary; assessing the status of children in families; offering rehabilitation of the child and family; and following up on cases at different levels. In addition, however, and more importantly, each CRRC is responsible for filling a major and serious gap in the Arab World in terms of conducting rigorous research studies and collecting statistical information and data on child abuse, neglect, labor, and any other kind of violation of children's rights. For, almost every single Arab country suffers from the lack of accurate statistics on incidence and prevalence of child abuse. This paucity of accurate statistics on violence against children is not only worrying but also "hinders the implementation of evidence-based prevention and intervention" (Al-Lamki, 2012; 2). One of its major consequences, as Al Eissa and Almuneef (2010) explain, is that "the risk factors, indicators, categories, definitions, and the nature of the problem of child maltreatment..[are]... not well identified and therefore, multidisciplinary services for the victims of abuse and their families...[are]...not well informed and developed..." (p.29). Another consequence is that although there may be a sense in most Arab countries that the situation concerning children's rights is improving, it remains difficult- because of the lack of data- to determine with accuracy the progress that has taken place. There is therefore a dire need for research in this area, in order to shed more light on the situation and to bring about positive changes in all its facets; since, based on the basic principle of quality assurance, without measurements, improving quality in any area is not possible. It follows, thus, that collecting accurate information and data on the prevalence and extent of abuse will have a direct and positive bearing on prevention of harm to children and on the treatment of the adults involved (Al-Lamki, 2012).

This service of conducting rigorous research to gain better comprehension of things is highly consistent with Quranic teachings that attribute high standing to those who are firmly grounded in knowledge and who seek understanding. It is true that most Quranic verses that uphold such teachings, like *Al-Imran (7)*, refer in specific to religious knowledge and understanding of the holy book but they are also usually interpreted in more general terms to encompass the seeking of knowledge and understanding of anything that can be studied. From an Islamic perspective, therefore, we have a duty to study, learn, investigate, and research to educate ourselves about things and be able to make informed decisions. Conducting rigorous research is what will constitute the value added to each CRRC and to the Ministry of Social Affairs under which they operate. Without it, matters will remain as they currently are, meaning attempts at the enforcement of child protection laws and conventions will continue to be weak, poorly informed, and below expectations.

It is very unfortunate that, up till now, research-focused centers such as the CRRC proposed here are not to be found anywhere in the Arab World. There seems to be currently only one center similar in objective and it is the *Center for Children's Rights* in Somaliland, for it is a research and action center which works to enhance adherence to the rights of the child; nevertheless, it is a non-governmental organization operated from abroad, while the framework here is calling for such centers to be run and funded by the government and to be an integral part of a nationwide social reform movement.

Ministry of Education

The Ministry of Education, under our framework, will have one of the most proactive roles with respect to protection of children's rights, in comparison to other ministries. The reason for this is that this ministry will focus on preparing whole generations of children in matters related to what their rights are, how to express them, what counts as a violation of them, and how to defend them. This is in addition to being involved in educating adults on the same things, as well as, training them on positive approaches for dealing with children. The main objective of the Ministry of Education therefore is to provide children with a set of skills that will empower them for the rest of their lives and not just to help them cope with and overcome a present and harmful situation. The focus therefore is ultimately on the outcomes or on what kind of graduates will be pumped into higher education institutions and/or society in the end of the K-12 formal education period. What is exactly expected of the Ministry of Education under our framework will be elaborated on in a separate chapter to come, because of its significance and substance.

With this explanation of the types of tasks the ministries will be engaged in during Lewin's second stage of change, we come next to the third and final phase in his model, which is known as the *Freezing* stage. At this point, every ministry and under the supervision of the CPAB will have to put together an action plan for celebrating the change it succeeds in bringing about, regardless of its magnitude. Every single step towards reform needs to be recognized, publicized, and rewarded in order to energize the troops on board and to motivate others- who are not- to join in the process. This action plan, therefore, will need to include steps for measuring and evaluating results of implemented projects, programs, and initiatives in order to: (1) recognize positive changes and thus celebrate them; (2) identify weaknesses and challenges and thus work on overcoming them; (3) determine opportunities and thus strategize how to take advantage of them; and finally, (4) pinpoint threats and proceed in obliterating them. When such an action plan is successfully implemented and with the right leadership support, feedback, and structural adaptations necessary, people will internalize the changes and begin using them in everyday activities, which will help develop in them a sense of stability and will increase their confidence levels in the new ways of doing things. Change, as a result, will become more anchored in each ministry and personnel will start getting work done more to full capacity, which will all be reflected positively on the children and adults they cater to. Without this freezing and its resulting constant change, sustainability of positive steps taken will be threatened and ministry personnel will not be psychologically nor practically ready to embrace any new change initiatives to follow (Evison, 2014). Constant positive change and sustainability of positive steps in the form of continuous direction towards what is right or good is even stressed on in the holy Quran and in several verses, like for example in *Taha (82)*, which states: *"But indeed, I am the Perpetual Forgiver of whoever repents and believes and does righteousness and then continues in guidance"*. There is also verse *Fussilat (30)*, which states: *"In the case of those who say, 'Our Lord is God', and, further, stand straight and steadfast... [continue in the right way]..., the angels descend on them (from time to time): 'Fear ye not!' (they suggest), 'Nor grieve! but receive the Glad Tidings of the Garden (of Bliss), that which ye were promised!'"*; and verse *Al-Ahqaf (13)*, which states: *"Verily those who say, 'Our*

Lord is God,' and remain firm (on that Path)...[continue in the right way]...,- on them shall be no fear, nor shall they grieve". The emphasis on continuity in righteousness and on treading the right path is obviously clear in these verses and although in this context they refer to what would lead to God Almighty, they nevertheless encompass what is good and right in general.

With this, we notice that the three stages of change prescribed by our framework all fit well with Islamic teachings, which is really an asset since this increases both the framework's plausibility and feasibility in Muslim Arab societies. For, while this framework is shaped by Lewin's organizational psychology and organizational development theory and concepts and thus caters to scientific-oriented minds, it is also well-supported by Islamic teachings and principles, to which the majority of Muslims are bound. This makes its acceptance therefore more plausible and widespread, especially if in the implementation of it, an emphasis is placed on making as many connections as possible between it and various Islamic values, *Hadiths*, and holy book verses. As was mentioned earlier in this book, the role and power of Islam in a Muslim's life should not be underestimated and in this case its binding power should be invested in, in order to bring about social positive change in the form of prevention of violation of children's rights. Such type of investment needs to be present at all levels in the framework, from the government to the CPAB to the ministries and their various directorates and departments to the CRRC spread out in different regions and provinces. For, without exception, one is capable of finding in Islamic teachings supporting evidence for almost every scientifically-based social or judicial or educational practice related to children and, thus, such an investment is very much viable and in place.

Chapter Eight

Education for Children's Rights

One essential ingredient for the protection of children's rights is education. The Ministry of Education (MOE) in any Arab country therefore has a chief responsibility upon its shoulders. As was pointed out in the previous chapter, it has one of the most proactive roles to be played; since by providing the right types of services, it can help in not only preventing violations of children's rights from existing adults but also in empowering generations of children intellectually, emotionally, morally, socially, religiously, and physically even from a very young age. This empowerment will help children learn how to defend themselves against abuse when young and will also prepare them to become caring and nurturing adults and parents of the future.

When spelled out, the role to be played by the MOE with respect to protection of children's rights is mainly this: its steering committee has to develop and implement a strategic plan that includes both (1) projects and programs that target adults who deal with children (e.g. teachers, parents, counselors, coaches, babysitters, etc.), and (2) projects and programs that target children themselves. For the implementation of this strategic plan to succeed, the MOE itself as an organization will have to go through phases similar to Lewin's *unfreeze, move, freeze* stages, in order to secure the occurrence of the necessary cultural and structural modifications; *buy-in* and action; and anchoring and sustainability of positive change. In other words, the ministry will have to start out with launching its own children's rights' awareness campaign, to emphasize the need for change and to help those working in it and around it re-examine their assumptions about children and the ways of dealing with them, in the hope that misconceptions get corrected and rectified. Second, it needs to involve its staff in the setting of a shared vision that is consistent with the government's *Children's Welfare Vision* and in the development of a mission statement and goals that help in the fulfillment of this vision. Next, it needs to execute action plans through which its goals and mission are achieved and then evaluate the taken actions, celebrate successes, and make adaptations when necessary, in order to anchor the positive changes and raise confidence levels, which eventually lead to greater and more advanced steps in the right direction. Of course, all of this- and at all levels- needs to be infused with, and supported by, Islamic principles, *Hadiths*, and Quranic verses to which people are strongly bound.

The MOE, in addition, needs to work with the Ministry of Justice on ensuring that no couple planning on getting married does so, before first obtaining a *parenting* certificate issued by the MOE and presented to the Ministry of Justice before validation of the marriage. This certificate would be similar in status to the premarital medical certificate required in most if not all Arab countries, without which a couple cannot get married. The only difference is that the latter is issued as a result of passing some medical tests and screening; whereas, the former would be issued only after the couple take an instructional short course on proper parenting and the avoidance of child abuse. Although this course by itself may not guarantee that all couples end up being good and nurturing parents, it nevertheless raises general awareness about children's rights and deprives adults, who falter in the future and commit violations during parenting, from the excuse of acting out of ignorance, when questioned about their inappropriate childrearing practices.

In addition to this instructional course targeting parents-to-be, the MOE needs to offer through its public and private schools similar courses to existing parents, teachers, and other professionals working with children in the communities they serve. These courses should focus primarily on the following areas: child development, different parenting styles and proper childrearing practices, character education, religious education, emotional intelligence, and ways of modeling positive alternative behaviors. Below is a brief discussion of what each area of focus should entail. Following it is a discussion of what areas of focus should be at the heart of programs targeting children themselves.

I. Programs Targeting Adults

Child Development

The greater the adults' knowledge about children's development in all aspects: physically, cognitively, emotionally, socially, morally, and spiritually, the more will they be prepared to understand children's needs and how they behave, think, learn, and feel and the greater their ability to interact with them positively. Studying development therefore is important since it helps guide adults' decisions about children's needs, environment, activities, and interactions.

Parenting Styles and Proper Parenting

Adults working with children need to be made aware of the different parenting styles that have been identified and recognized by psychologists in the research literature, in order to be able to assess, identify, and modify- if need be- their own parenting style. The work of the renowned psychologist Diana Baumrind comes to mind here and precisely her Parenting Styles Model, which was based on two main dimensions of parenting, known as *parental responsiveness* and *parental demandingness*. The first refers to how much the parents respond to their children's needs; whereas, the latter refers to how much maturity and responsibility they expect back from their children. Baumrind's model used these two aspects to identify three different parenting styles, which are the following (Baumrind, 1966):

- Authoritarian: This style is known as the style that is *too hard*. These parents are highly demanding and are not responsive enough to their children's needs. They tend to be controlling and favor punitive measures to restrict children's autonomy. They do not allow for verbal give and take and are harsh and rigid in enforcing their rules. Parents who abuse their children tend to be of this style; although, not all authoritarian parents are abusive.
- Permissive: This style is known as the style that is *too soft*. These parents are highly responsive to their children but are very low on being demanding. They do not use punitive measures and are usually accepting of their children's desires, impulses, and actions. They tend, as a result, to spoil their children, without exercising much control over them, while allowing them to regulate their own activities as much as possible.
- Authoritative: This style is known as being *just right*. These parents are high on being both demanding and responsive. They are firm in dealing with their children but are at the same time caring and encourage interaction, dialogue, and verbal give and take with them. This leads to the parents being flexible with their children and willing to make exceptions based on the situation.

Baumrind made it clear in her studies that the authoritative style of parenting is superior to all other styles and there is general consensus in the literature over this. This style is what all parents should aim for and should be trained to adopt; for, it constitutes one of the main building blocks in laying the foundation for effective childrearing practices. This style should also act as a model for other adults working with children. Teachers, in particular, need to be trained to use it as an example to be followed in their classroom management techniques. When compared to the other styles, this style in particular guarantees that children are responsible and disciplined as should, while simultaneously being loved and cared for and having their rights protected, respected, and granted.

Character Education

The objective here is not to train adults on implementing a specific character education program with clearly defined values and pillars, which may succeed and which may not. Instead, the objective is twofold: (1) to educate adults about the distinction between *values education* and *character education* and (2) to explain to them that to bring up disciplined children, the former alone is insufficient. For, if we look at education and childrearing practices in the Arab World, we notice that there seems to be a lot of emphasis on the indoctrination of values. Such indoctrination, in most part, is done not only at home but also through the different religious studies classes that students take in school or religious lessons and speeches (*khutab*) that take place in mosques or in similar religious gatherings. The result of such indoctrination is that most if not all children in the Arab World usually know very well how to theoretically differentiate between right and wrong, good and bad, socially acceptable and socially unacceptable, religiously prohibited *(haram)* and religiously permissible *(halal)*. When it comes to practice, however, we notice that Arab societies, like many other parts of the world, are faced with the challenge of moral decline and the need for revitalizing moral and ethical values and their reflection in daily practices (Rassekh, 2001). Certainly, there are well-behaved Arab children who are brought up to respect and abide by moral values; simultaneously, however, there are increasingly many who lie, cheat, swear, steal, break promises, vandalize, deceive, disobey rules, bully others etc., even though they very well know that such actions are immoral. A pressing question is why do children behave in such unethical ways when they happen to know better? Part of the problem has to do with the ways they are being brought up, which focus mainly on values inculcation instead of focusing on developing in them moral habits that lead to a genuine moral character. In other words, there seems to be in childrearing practices in families and schools in the Arab World, a deficiency in character education, which helps children develop as personal and social beings; for, such kind of education is not only keen on instilling moral values in children but also on developing their social, emotional, and cognitive skills, as well as their critical thinking, moral reasoning, life skills, and peaceful conflict resolution abilities. Such development which constitutes the formation of the moral character consists according to Lickona (1996) of three main stages, which are: moral knowing, moral doing, and moral feeling. What this means is that for children to both *know* and *do* what is morally right and avoid doing the morally wrong, they need to be (1) taught right from wrong and good from bad (*i.e. values education*); (2) repeatedly provided with opportunities to act morally; and (3) trained to value what is right or good and to appreciate acting according to it and committing themselves deeply to it.

When adults are trained in teaching children in this way and from a very young age, they guarantee the upbringing of ethically responsible and well-disciplined children who gradually develop internal sanctions that prevent them from doing wrong and, consequently, develop the habits of acting morally consistently. The need therefore for using any form of harsh punishment with such children, *as discipline*, gets evaded. This in turn abates unacceptable dealings with children and violations of their rights, that are commonly committed under the name of 'disciplining a child'. It also guarantees, in general, the generation of better and more righteous citizens and parents who possess the internal sanctions needed to prevent them from harming their own future children.

Religious Education

On the same lines as character education, the focus should not only be on the explanation of the main pillars and values of

Islam but rather on the opportunities given to practice them. The best example here is how Muslim families get their children to pray five times a day out of true conviction. This does not get actualized except (1) when the parents themselves act as good role models and complete their daily prayers; (2) when the children are not only told and advised to pray but are also trained to actually get up and pray or even go to the mosque every time they hear the call for prayer; and (3) through proper follow-up and reinforcement of children's attempts at completing their daily prayers. Explaining to children the benefits of praying, therefore, or advising them to pray, usually does not alone suffice to get them to fulfill this essential Islamic pillar. Similarly, the same applies for all the other Islamic values, teachings, and duties. As was explained in Chapter 1 of this book, this type of education consisting of (1) modeling true Islamic values and teachings, (2) providing the related training not only on how and when to act but also on reasoning practically and deliberating about why to act in such a way and what is required in a particular situation, and (3) following up on children's performance and actions, usually results in- *with repetition*- the development of the true Islamic character, which if formed, will be characterized by the essential Islamic values of peace, forgiveness, mercy, compassion, selflessness, humility, kindness, generosity, good treatment, and good deeds.

When adults are trained on delivering such type of religious education to children through the programs offered by the MOE, they may get the opportunity to discover glitches in the ways they themselves were religiously brought up. They may also realize imperfections in their own practices with their children and make wise decisions to correct them. This would naturally and consequently lead to improved religious upbringing and to better behavior from their children's side, all of which would protect the latter from any kind of mistreatment and violations.

In addition, adults need to be reminded of the rights Islam grants to children and of the Islamic emphasis on respecting them. Referring to specific examples of how the Prophet Muhammad *(Peace be upon him)* and his followers used to deal with children and care for their well-being, not only physically but also emotionally, would come in very handy here. One famous example is the story of when a little child, who was sitting in the lap of Prophet Muhammad *(Peace be upon him)*, accidentally urinated and his father got extremely embarrassed and, as a result, scolded him. The Prophet then calmed the father down and told him that what had happened was no big issue, since his clothes could be washed easily. He strongly urged the father, however, to be more careful with how he treats his child; since, what is it that could restore the child's self-esteem after being dealt with in public in this harsh way (Kassamali, 1998)? Stories such as these indicate Islam's keenness on protecting children from harm- *even if it were just harm caused by an unthoughtful word in a time of anger-* and its assertion as a religion of a child's right to being handled with care.

Emotional Intelligence

Emotional intelligence can be defined as a "subset of social intelligence that involves the ability to monitor one's own and others' feelings and emotions, to discriminate among them and to use this information to guide one's thinking and actions" (Salovey & Mayer, 1990; 189). It involves recognizing, perceiving, reasoning with, understanding, and managing our emotions, in addition to, understanding and empathizing with the emotions of others, in order to relate to them better and build stronger relationships with them. Emotional intelligence thus consists of a number of abilities among them self-awareness, self-management, motivation, empathy, and social skills. By offering training courses and workshops for adults to improve their emotional intelligence abilities, the MOE helps them learn how to control their emotions better, manage their stress levels, and replace their negative reactions with more positive ones when dealing with children. Such training also enables adults to see things from children's perspectives and to identify with them more, which leads to avoiding conflicts with them before they even start; it also makes adults better at negotiation because of their understanding of what others, and in this context children, need and want. With lesser conflicts and greater empathy towards children, certainly the result is a drop in children's rights violations.

Modeling Positive Alternative Behaviors

There is a growing body of literature that indicates that "parents' own aggressive problem solving strategies have implications for the children's aggressive and assertive problem solutions with peers" (Duman & Margolin, 2007; p. 54). Children, therefore, usually tend to follow in their parents' footsteps when it comes to ways of approaching matters, solving problems, and resolving conflicts. If the parents, therefore, regularly exhibit negative behaviors in such dealings, the children will most probably do the same, since they would not have been exposed nor accustomed to any other alternative behaviors. In other words, they would not know any better. The end result for the child, consequently, is usually some form of verbal or physical punishment- or even abuse- because parents and/or teachers are not willing to tolerate what gets labeled as "misbehavior" on the part of the child, when it really is only an imitation of the parents' negative behaviors. One way of reducing the chances of children getting punished and abused, therefore, is by adults modeling for them- and from the beginning- positive alternative behaviors when resolving conflicts, finding solutions to problems, and even handling daily hassles. Such types of positive behaviors, however, do not always come naturally and most of the time need to be acquired through training and practice. For this reason, courses and workshops that provide professionals working with children with both the theoretical as well as the practical knowledge needed for the acquisition of such positive alternative behaviors, should be made available by the MOE.

II. Programs Targeting Children

With respect to the MOE programs that target children, they need to focus on the following areas, which will be explained separately and in detail below: human and children's rights, integrated and infused curricula, religious education, moral education, habits of mind, emotional intelligence, personal development, personal counseling, and reflection.

Human Rights with a Focus on Children's Rights

Students in schools need to be provided with courses that educate them about what their rights are, how to express them, what counts as a violation of them, and how to defend them. They need to be taught such things through a lot of examples and case studies. They should also be educated about human rights in general and human duties, so that they can understand better why adults behave the way they do and can learn to discriminate between when adults are acting from a sense of duty stemming from their position of authority on the one hand, and when they are possibly abusing their position and using it to encroach on the rights of others, mainly the children they deal with, on the other. In addition, children need to be taught about their own duties towards adults, so that they can act accordingly, without trying too hard to please *at any expense* those who deal with them, including the expense of sometimes having their rights breached. Courses like these also need to guide children regarding what type of treatment to accept and what not to and need to provide them with information like whom to contact, when to contact, and how to contact, when in danger or under any kind of threat.

Integrated/Infused Curricula

In addition to offering independent courses that focus on children's rights, as described above, the MOE needs to develop all its curricula in ways that subtly incorporate examples, messages, lessons, objectives, activities, and assessments that affirm the rights of the child. The traditional curricula taught in schools, therefore, with the different subject matter they focus on, need to be infused with content and practical opportunities that allow students to explore, discuss, think critically about, and experiment with their rights and what may be violations of them. Through such infused curricula, students should also be given the opportunity to learn to value and appreciate their rights as divine, sacred, and worthy of protection. The MOE should also require schools to include extracurricular activities and clubs that promote understanding of the concept of 'rights', in general, and the concept of 'children's rights', in particular, and its implementation.

Religious Education

As was explained earlier in this book, the primary objective of religious education should be the development of children's true Islamic character. As was elaborated before, this gets actualized with adults modeling for children true Islamic values and teachings, children repeatedly practicing behaving in a deliberative Islamic manner, and adults providing in return the necessary feedback. Developing such a character in children leads to better behavior from their side, which helps ensure that adults are not left with any excuse for abusing children under the veiled name of 'discipline'. Looking at the way religious education is delivered in the Muslim Arab World, we notice that it is mainly normative in nature, in the sense that it prescribes for us- as children- how one should act, speak, live, treat others, etc. It is true that all these prescriptions, if followed correctly, guarantee sensitivity to and respect of the rights of others. Still, however, they do not always make explicitly clear to us what we ourselves should expect from others and how *we* as children should be treated. In other words, they do not openly describe what our rights are and it is unsurprising to find some children and even adults who are not very conscious of the extent of rights they were granted divinely. For this reason, as a result, the MOE needs to reexamine the religious studies curricula taught in its schools and shift the focus of some of their parts from prescribing for children how they should treat others to describing for them instead how they should be treated in ways that guarantee respect for their rights.

Moral Education

As was stressed upon before, the type of moral education needed in the Arab World is mainly character education, which helps children develop as personal and social beings. From a very young age, therefore, students need to be trained and exposed in their classes, courses, and activities to opportunities that allow them to not only acquire the right type of moral values but also to: (1) develop their social, emotional, and cognitive skills; (2) exercise their critical thinking, moral reasoning, life skills, and peaceful conflict resolution abilities to make the correct ethical judgments and decisions; (3) act according to the socially accepted ethical standards and code of conduct; and (4) develop deep appreciation of and commitment to acting according to what is right and avoiding what is wrong. Again here, these types of opportunities need to be provided in the form of both separate curricula devoted for the teaching of ethical values and ethical behavior and also infused curricula and extra-curricular activities and clubs.

This type of education with its positive outcomes somewhat helps ensure protection of children from abusive behavior disguised under the name of 'discipline'. Thinking and acting morally therefore can act as a shield against violations of a child's rights and so it is something that is in their best interest. For children to be able to think and act in this particular way, though, they need to possess a certain cognitive structure and need to be equipped with certain cognitive skills; for, as the renowned psychologist Jean Piaget explained, moral development is greatly influenced by- and depends on- cognitive development (Dworetzky,1995). The more cognitively advanced children are and the more developed they are in their critical thinking, logical reasoning, problem solving, decision making and conflict resolution skills, the more prepared they can be to think, deliberate, and act morally. Adults dealing with children, therefore, mainly teachers in this context, have a responsibility to train children as much as possible on such higher-order thinking skills, through their different lessons and activities, in order to help empower them to become effective moral actors.

Habits of Mind

In order to protect themselves against others who may try to abuse their rights in any way, children are in need of being equipped with the tools, resources, and skills needed to help them (1) analyze situations better, (2) detect possible dangers, risks, and threatening cues in them, and (3) make decisions about how to act or react toward them. Such tools and resources consist of critical and creative thinking skills which, according to Costa and Kallick (2008), are usually developed through a set of thinking dispositions known as 'habits of mind'. These dispositions or habits are characteristic of what intelligent people do when they are faced with complex problems and challenges, whose solutions are not directly apparent, and they help individuals in regulating their thinking and learning.

The MOE, as a result, has a responsibility to provide children with opportunities that help develop and promote in them such habits of mind from a young age. Out of the 16 habits of mind specified by Costa and Kallick (2008), the habits of 'gathering data through all the senses', 'applying past knowledge to new situations', and 'taking responsible risks' are especially important in this context, since they can help children develop their ability of sensing dangers and threats and acting against them. The opportunities provided by the MOE should focus on infused lessons that consist of subject matter content, objectives, activities, and assessment that are permeated with higher order thinking skills, mainly critical, logical, and creative thinking, all of which deepen children's comprehension and understanding and equip them better in the face of any potential harm.

Personal Development and Emotional Intelligence

Helping children develop personally is expected from all schools and, usually, schools that are distinguished in meeting this expectation focus, among other things, on: helping children set their own realistic goals and plan for their achievement; promoting their self-concept and self-esteem; helping them identify, understand, and regulate their feelings and emotions, and increasing their self-motivation. To help children in the protection and realization of their rights, however, children need to be provided with assertiveness training, the goals of which are not only to make children more aware of their personal rights but also to teach them how to communicate and express them forthrightly away from ineffective passive and aggressive responses (Goleman, 1996). For, aggressive communication usually entails judging others harshly or threatening them or even violating their rights and boundaries; while the passive one, on the other hand, allows others to victimize us and act aggressively towards us and, consequently, this may later on eventually result in a vicious comeback from our side against the aggressor (Mellody, Miller, & Miller, 2003). Both types of communication, however, can lead to a weakened self-respect and can also put a child more at risk of abusive behavior from adults. Since, aggressive communication could be perceived as misbehavior and may, therefore, aggravate the adults dealing with the child causing them to react violently against them; while, passive communication could render the child to be perceived as vulnerable and weak and, as a result, to be thought of as an easy target. The positive mean between the two types is self-assertiveness and this particular aspect of personal development is exactly what the MOE should compel schools to develop in children through a variety of specific courses, instructional activities, and extracurricular events. This is in addition to developing children's emotional intelligence, which can help them monitor and discriminate between their different feelings and emotions as well as between the different feelings and emotions exhibited by adults. This discrimination is extremely useful since it helps guide their thinking and actions (Salovey & Mayer, 1990). It also helps them understand and empathize more with the emotions of the adults who deal with them, and thus build stronger bonds and relationships between the two.

Personal Counseling

Students in school need to be provided from a young age with counseling services, to improve their coping skills, self-esteem, problem-solving capacities, self-management, assertiveness and communication skills, and general outlook on life. Such services also help them manage their stress, build better relationships with others, make more informed decisions, define their goals, and achieve personal success. All of these benefits make children more equipped and prepared to not succumb to the negative effects of abuse, when it happens, and to notice it and its signals and protect oneself from it before it does take place. Such counseling services in schools can particularly support children going through traumatic experiences like abuse, in ways that not only make them survive their trauma but also prosper through it and thrive.

Reflection

Training children from a young age to reflect on their own experiences and learn from them can prove to be extremely beneficial especially in cases of maltreatment. This is due to the fact that examining and exploring one's experiences rather than just living them helps in developing higher order thinking skills like critical and creative thinking, which are important for problem-solving and conflict resolution. John Dewey (1993), who is well-known for stating that we do not learn from experience but rather from reflecting on experience, considered reflection as a type of problem-solving through which several ideas are connected with each other to promote more complex and interrelated ideas that lead to the resolution of some issue. Reflection, therefore, as an exercise, should be generally practiced by all and in all classes and activities in school, until it becomes a common practice. It is true that an abused child may not be able to rid their self of the abuse they are being subjected to through reflection; however, with such a strategy and under the supervision of the school psychologist or counselor or social worker, the child can be trained to (1) consider a past maltreatment incident, (2) think about what strategies were used in it for protection or coping, (3) identify personal strengths and possible resources that could have been utilized to face such an incident, and (4) wonder about what was learned and what could be done differently to combat possible future incidents. These four steps of how children should be trained to reflect upon their traumatic experiences are inspired by the original steps proposed by the positive psychologist and resilience specialist Dr. Christopher Johnstone (2010) in his non-medication treatment for depression model, better known as the *Medication-free SSRI* (Strategies, Strengths, Resources, and Insights). The significance of such reflection training is that it can help children avoid getting trapped in the fear, self-defeat, and depressive state they usually experience, due to the stressful abuse they are subjected to, and instead focus on finding more positive ways of thinking about themselves and their abilities in a manner that helps them transition to a more sustainable way of life and realize that the delinquency and flaw is not in them but rather in the one abusing them.

Reflection, in general, is an anciently called-for practice. It is as old as the philosophies of Plato, Aristotle, and Confucius.

In addition, it is a practice highly praised and required in the teachings of the holy Quran. Plenty of verses refer to it, like: *Al-Baqarah 219* and *266, Al-Imran 191, An-nisaa 82, Al-Anam 50, Al-A'raf 176* and *184, Yunus 24, Ar-ra`d 3, An-nahl 11, 44,* and *69, Ar-rum 21, Az-zumar 42, Al-jathiyah 13,* and many others. It is surprising therefore that it has not been sufficiently emphasized, if at all, in the educational systems and religious studies of the Muslim Arab World. Only recently have we started hearing new and young Muslim Arab scholars emphasizing its significance as a practice and only because they have received their education in- or have been influenced by- the West or Southeast Asian countries like Singapore and Malaysia, which are relatively advanced in their systems of education. It is about time, therefore, to waken up this essential practice, which is even older than our religion, from its everlasting slumber and revive it in such a way that it becomes a part of each and every individual's routine and habits of mind. With it, we can improve many aspects of our lives, whether personal or social or professional, and at all levels. To become proficient in such a practice, however, training from a young age at home and in schools is needed, which if provided, would contribute to the betterment of an individual's life and to the betterment of the community (*um'ma*) as a whole.

With this elaborate but substantial account of what types of programs are to be offered by the MOE, the explanation of our proposed framework comes to an end. This framework was never originally intended as an ideal solution for child abuse in the Muslim Arab World, if at all there is such a thing as an ideal solution. Rather, it was intended from the initial stages of its formation to be at least a workable solution and if this framework gets implemented correctly, has a great potential to at least reduce the magnitude of the problem of child abuse from which all countries in the world suffer, although at varying scales. The characteristics that increase this framework's chances of success are outlined in the subsequent concluding chapter.

Chapter Nine

Concluding Remarks

This book attempted to cover the issue of child abuse in the Muslim Arab World in all its facets. It did so by both taking a descriptive approach as well as a prescriptive one. On the one hand, it tried to describe the rights granted to children in Islam; the actual status of children's rights in the Muslim Arab World and the region's position towards international children's rights conventions; types of violations of children's rights and abuse existing in the region; possible explanations of why such violations exist; causes and effects of child abuse and neglect in general; child custody and the prevalence in the Arab World of a neglected area of emotional abuse known as parental alienation; the relationship between mental illness and child abuse; and actual cases of child maltreatment extracted from news reports from the region. On the other hand, it endeavored to prescribe how child protection and prevention of abuse could be practically ensured to a higher degree in the Muslim Arab World and what crucial role could be played by education in the process. It did so by proposing a practical framework characterized by several factors that make it plausible, feasible, as well as, appealing. Of the most prominent of these factors are the following:

- *The Humanitarian Factor*: The framework has as its purpose a fundamental human issue and is concerned with the alleviation of suffering and with improving the welfare not only of little children but also of society as a whole. It is therefore a framework that can be found appealing by any individual who possesses in their heart compassion and kindness for other humans in general. The advantage of this framework is that it has the potential to create and strengthen effective advocacy for breaking the silence and, therefore, adopting active compassion instead, against violence, injustice, harm, injury, and maltreatment done to the innocent and vulnerable but right-bearing children of today and the fathers and mothers of the future.

- *The Contextualization Factor*: The framework is not developed in abstraction but rather is positioned in and bounded by a specific culture, religion, and social context. It was originally born out of (1) true and actual stories and reports of child abuse and neglect; (2) tangible binding forces and practices mainly religious and cultural in nature that impact individuals in almost every aspect of their lives; and (3) factually collected data and research regardless of how limited they may be. All of this adds to the framework's relevance to the party it directly targets- and for whom it was originally developed- and also increases its feasibility in the eyes of other secondarily intended groups. In brief, positioning the framework in this way, brings it more to life and makes it more proximal to the experiences and lives of others.

- *The Multidimensionality Factor:* The proposed framework is anything but limited in perspective; for it does not just focus on one key player or on one aspect of personal and social development. Rather, it involves a number of key players (i.e. different governmental entities like CPAB, ministries, the CRRC, hospitals, courts, schools, police stations, etc.) and aims at educating and developing individuals personally, socially, emotionally, intellectually, morally, and spiritually, in addition to developing the community as a whole. The end result is a comprehensive framework capable of satisfying the desire of any intelligent mind and providing a solidly aligned roadmap ready for implementation by any positive and forceful initiator of social change.

- *The Interdisciplinary Factor:* The framework, with all its principles and propositions, also hinges on and draws from several branches of learning or fields of expertise, mainly: philosophy, psychology, managerial sciences, religion, and education. It also relies in many instances on statistical data and reviews of research findings. This helps in shedding more light on- and in guaranteeing a deeper and more profound understanding of- the complexity of the issue of child abuse in the Muslim Arab World. It also guarantees a more robust tackling of the problem under examination. Although all in all beneficial, such an interdisciplinary approach is of great interest especially to governmental agencies and professional organizations that are both aware and appreciate the advantages of systems thinking for tackling complex issues and problems.
- *The Compositeness Factor:* The proposed framework, like this whole book, is composite in that it subtly manages to combine Arabic and Islamic perspectives and realities on the one hand with Western theories, models, and scientific research data on the other. In a way, it is a successful marriage between East and West. It is true that its main focus is on the Muslim Arab World; still, it is a framework that can prove to be beneficial to other social contexts similar in their socioeconomic development level, cultural peculiarities, and common problems.

These factors, as well as others that are not mentioned here, are what distinguish the proposed framework. This framework happens to be the main contribution aimed for by this book; since, rather than simply describing how things are, it outlines for us exactly what it is we need to do to bring about some form of positive social change. It acts therefore as a light leading the way for us and guiding us to actually be humanitarian in actions and deeds and not only in thoughts and emotions. More importantly, it acts as the means needed to give children in the Muslim Arab World a voice- a voice that has sadly been in many, if not in most, cases buried under the sand covering so much of our desert lands. With it, children in every country in the region can rest assured that there is still hope for them for a dignified life, by having a well-defined and unified national strategy that aims at their protection and at defending their divine rights. With it, finally, we can guarantee that our children will look after us in our old age and treat us as cherished beings worthy of mercy and care, in exactly the same way they had been treated when little. Only then, can our children- while standing between the merciful hands of God- faithfully, resolutely, and confidently recite in their prayers for us *their parents* (or whoever is of equal standing) the second part of the Quranic verse *Al-isra'a (24):*

> *"My Lord! Bestow on them thy Mercy,*
> *as they cherished me in childhood."*

References

Aboul-Hagag, K.E. & Hamed, A.F. (2012). Prevalence and pattern of child sexual abuse reported by cross sectional study among the University students, Sohag University, Egypt. *Egyptian Journal of Forensic Sciences.* 2, 89-96.

Adams, P. (2011). In Lebanon, mental health is on the mend. *World Report.* 377, 707-708.

Ahmed, A.S. (1998). *Islam today.* London: I.B. Tauris Publishers.

Al Eissa, M. & Almuneef, M. (2010). Child abuse and neglect in Saudi Arabia: Journey of recognition to implementation of national prevention strategies. *Child Abuse and Neglect.* 34, 28-33.

Al-Ghamidi, M. (2004). Custody of child after divorce. *Islam Today.* Retrieved 4 February 2014, from http://en.islamtoday.net/quesshow-22-1006.htm.

Al-Ghamidi, M. (2011). Exceptions in custody cases must be handled by an Islamic judge. *Islam Online 2011.* Retrieved 5 February 2014, from http://www.islamonline.com/news/articles/135/Custody-of-child-after-divorce.html.

Al-Hargan, A. (2005). Saudi Arabia and the international covenant on civil and political rights 1966: A stalemate situation. *The International Journal of Human Rights.* 9(4), 491-505.

Al-Hayani, F.A. (2007). Biomedical ethics: Muslim perspectives on genetic modification. *Zygon: Journal of Religion & Science.* 42(1), 153-162.

Al- Lamki, L. (2012). Child rights: What can we do in Oman? *Sultan Qaboos University Medical Journal.* 12(1), 1-4.

Al-Sheha, A. (1997). *Women in the shade of Islam.* Riyadh, KSA: Islamic Propagation Office in Rabwah.

Ali, A. (1995). Cultural discontinuity in Arab management thought. *International Studies in Management and Organization.* 25(3), 7-30.

Ali, A., Gibbs, M. and Camp, R.C. (2003). Jihad in monotheistic religions: Implications for business and management. *International Journal of Sociology and Social Policy.* 23(12), 19-42.

Ali, A.Y. (Translator) (2009). *The Holy Quran: Text and Translation.* New York: The Other Press.

Ali, M.M. (2005). The Islamic revivalist perspective of development. *Canadian Journal of Development Studies.* 26(2), 275-291.

Al-Krenawi, A., Lev-Wiesel, R., and Mahmud, A.S. (2007). Psychological symptomatology among Palestinian adolescents living with political violence. *Child and Adolescent Mental Health.* 12(1), 27-31

Al-Mahroos, F., Abdulla, F., Kamal, S., Al-Ansari, A. (2005). Child abuse: Bahrain's experience. *Child Abuse and Neglect.* 29, 187-193.

Abdullah, A. (2014). The Prophet's compassion for children. *Mission Islam.* Retrieved 1 March, 2014, from: http://www.missionislam.com/family/prophetscompassion.htm

American Psychological Association official website. Retrieved 16 August, 2009, from: http://www.apa.org/ppo/issues/capta-reauthorization-recommendations.pdf.

Arab Organization for Human Rights. (1990). Human rights in the Arab World. *Arab Studies Quarterly.* 12(3/4), 103-124.

Armstrong, K. (2006). *Muhammad: Prophet for our time.* London: Harper Press.

Baker, A.J. (2005). The long-term effects of parental alienation on adult children: A qualitative research study. *The American Journal of Family Therapy.* 33(4), 289-302.

Baker, A.J. (2007). *Adult children of parental alienation syndrome.* New York, NY: W.W. Norton and Company.

Baker, A.J. and Ben-Ami, N. (2011). To turn a child against a parent is to turn a child against himself: The direct and indirect effects of exposure to parental alienation strategies on self-esteem and well-being. *Journal of Divorce and Remarriage.* 52(7), 472-489.

Baumrind, D. (1966). Effects of Authoritative Parental Control on Child Behavior, *Child Development, 37(4),* 887-907.

Becker-Weidman, A. & Hughes, D. (2008). Dyadic developmental psychotherapy: an evidence-based treatment for children with complex trauma and disorders of attachment. *Child and Family Social Work.* 13, 329-337.

Beckett, S. (1954). *Waiting for Godot.* New York: Grove Press.

Ben-Ami, N. and Baker, A.J.L. (2012). The long-term correlates of childhood exposure to parental alienation on adult self-sufficiency and well-being. *The American Journal of Family Therapy.* 40(2), 169-183.

Bener, A. and Ghuloum, S. (2011). Ethnic differences in the knowledge, attitude and beliefs towards mental illness in a traditional fast developing country. *Psychiatria Danubina.* 23(2), 157-164.

Bone, J.M. and Walsh, M.R. (1999). Parental alienation syndrome: How to detect it and what to do about it. *The Florida Bar Journal.* 73(3), 44-48.

Boston University School of Medicine, (2012). *Islam and Health.* Retrieved 19 February, 2014, from the Boston Healing Landscape Project website at: http://www.bu.edu/bhlp/Resources/Islam/health/illness.html

Bradbury, H., Mirvis, P., Neilsen, E., & Pasmore, W. (2007). Action Research at Work: Creating the Future Following the Path from Lewin. In P. Reason and H. Bradbury, *The SAGE Handbook of Action Research: Participative Inquiry and Practice.* (2nd ed.), (pp.77-92). Thousand Oaks: Sage Publications.

Bremner, J., Southwick, S., Johnson, D., Yehuda, R., Charney, D. (1993). Childhood physical abuse and combat-related post-traumatic stress disorder in Vietnam veterans. *American Journal of Psychiatry.* 150, 235-239.

Caddy, G.R. (2013). Review of "Working with alienated children and families: A clinical guidebook, " edited by Amy J.L. Baker and S. Richard Sauber. *The American Journal of Family Therapy.* 41(4), 361-362.

Chaffin, M., Kelleher, K., and Hollenberg, J. (1996). Onset of physical abuse and neglect: Psychiatric substance abuse, and social risk factors from prospective community data. *Child Abuse and Neglect.* 20(3), 191-203.

Chase, A. & Hamzawy, A. (Ed.). (2006). *Human rights in the Arab World: Independent voices.* Philadelphia, PA, USA: University of Pennsylvania Press.

Childinfo: Monitoring the Situation of Children and Women webpage. UNICEF official website. Retrieved 21 February, 2013, from: http://www.childinfo.org/protection.html

Childress, C.A. (2013). *Reconceptualizing Parental Alienation: Parental Personality Disorder and the Transgenerational Transmission of Attachment Trauma.* Retrieved 25 February, 2014, from: http://www.drcachildress.org/asp/admin/getFile. asp?RID=69&TID=6&FN=pdf.

Collngs, S. & Davies, L. (2008). For the sake of the children: Making sense of children and childhood in the context of child protection. *Journal of Social Work Practice.* 22 (2), 181-193.

Convention on the Rights of the Child (CRC) webpage. UNICEF official website. Retrieved 16 August, 2013, from: http://www. unicef.org/rightsite/237_202.htm

Costa, A.L. and Kallick, B. (Eds.).(2008). *Learning and leading with habits of mind.* Virginia, USA: Association for Supervision and Curriculum Development (ASCD).

Crabtree, S.A. (2007). Maternal perceptions of care-giving of children with developmental disabilities in the United Arab Emirates. *Journal of Applied Research in Intellectual Disabilities.* 20, 247-255.

Crabtree, S.A. (2008). Dilemmas in international social work education in the United Arab Emirates: Islam, localization and social need. *Social Work Education.* 27 (5), 536-548.

Cuffe, S.P., McCullough, E.L., Parmariega, A.J. (1994). Comorbidity of attention deficit hyperactivity disorder and posttraumatic stress disorder. *Journal of Child and Family Studies.* 3, 327-336.

Cupoli, J.M. & Newberger, E.H. (1977). Optimism or pessimism for the victim of child abuse? *Pediatrics.* 59 (2), 311-314.

Dewey, J. (1933). *How we think: A restatement of the relation of reflecting thinking to the educative process.* Boston: D.C. Heath.

Dong, M., Anda, R., Felitti, V., Dube, S., Williamson, D., Thompson, T., Loo, C., and Giles, W. (2004). The interrelatedness of multiple forms of childhood abuse, neglect, and household dysfunction. *Child Abuse and Neglect.* 28, 771-784.

Drozd, L.M. & Olesen, N.W. (2004) Is it abuse, alienation, and/or estrangement? *Journal of Child Custody.* 1(3), 65-106.

Dube, S. Anda, R., Felitti, V., Croft, J., Edwards, V., and Gile, W. (2001). Growing up with parental alcohol abuse: Exposure to childhood abuse, neglect, and household dysfunction. *Child Abuse and Neglect.* 25, 1627-1640.

Duman, S. & Margolin, G. (2007). Parents' aggressive influences and children's aggressive problem solutions with peers. *Journal of Clinical Child and Adolescent Psychology.* 36 (1), 42-55.

Dworetzky, J.P. & Davis, N.J. (1995). *A life span approach* (2nd ed.). Colorado, USA: West Publishing Company.

Erickson, M. & Egeland, B. (2002). Child neglect. In *The APSAC Handbook on Child Maltreatment.* (2nd ed.). Edited by J. Myers et al. Thousand Oaks, CA: Sage Publications.

Esposito, J.L. (2005). *Islam: The straight path* (Revised 3rd ed.). Oxford: Oxford University Press.

Evison, A. (2014). *Lewin's change management model: Understanding the three stages of change.* Retrieved 18 March, 2014, from: http://www.mindtools.com/pages/article/newPPM_94.htm.

Fakunmoju, S.B., Bammeke, F.O., Bosaikoh, T.A., Asante, R.K.B., Wooten, N.R., Hill, A.C., and Karpman, H. (2013). Perception and determination of child maltreatment: Exploratory comparisons across three countries. *Children and Youth Services Review.* 35, 1418-1430.

Finzi, R., Cohen, O., Sapir, Y., and Weizman, A. (2000) Attachment styles in maltreated children: a comparative study. *Child Development and Human Development.* 31, 113-128.

Fleming, J., Mullen, P.E., Sibthorpe, B., and Bammer, G. (1999). The long-term impact of childhood sexual abuse in Australian women. *Child Abuse & Neglect.* 23, 145-159.

Freeman, M.D.A., (1999). A child's right to circumcision. *BJU International.* 83(1), 74-78.

Gagne, M.H., Drapeau, S., Melancon, C., Saint-Jacques, M.C., and Lepine, R. (2007). Links between parental psychological violence, other family disturbances, and children's adjustment. *Family Process.* 46(4), 523-542.

Gardner, R.A. (2002). Parental alienation syndrome vs. parental alienation: Which diagnosis should evaluators use in child-custody disputes? *The American Journal of Family Therapy.* 30, 93-115.

Gardner, R.A. (2003). Does DSM-IV have equivalents for the parental alienation syndrome (PAS) diagnosis? *American Journal of Family Therapy.* 31(1), 1-21.

Gauther, D.P. (1963). *Practical reasoning.* Oxford: The Clarendon Press.

Glaser, D. (2000). Child abuse and neglect and the brain: A review. *Journal of Child Psychology and Psychiatry.* 41(1), 97-116.

Graham, T. (1993). Beyond detection: education and the abused student. *Social Work in Education.* 15(4), 197-206.

Goleman, D. (1996). *Emotional Intelligence.* London: Bloomsbury Publishing Plc.

Halwani, T.M. (2008). Is child abuse only restricted in medical practice? What about the rest of the society? *The Internet Journal of Health.* 7(2).

Hammad, S.H. (1999). The CRC: 'Words on paper' or a reality for children-A case study of Jordan. *International Journal of Children's Rights.* 7 (3), 215-237.

Ibrahim, N.K.R., Jalali, E.A.E., Al-Ahmadi, J., and Al-Bar, A.A. (2008). Prevalence, risk factors and outcome of childhood abuse reported by female university students in Jeddah. *Journal of Egypt Public Health Association.* 83(5,6), 329-351.

Irwin, T.H. (1980). The metaphysical and psychological basis of Aristotle's ethics. In A.O. Rorty (Ed.), *Essays on Aristotle's Ethics* (pp.35-53). California: University of California Press.

Jankowski,M.K., Leitenberg, H., Henning, K., and Coffey, P. (2002). Parental caring as a possible buffer against sexual revictimization in young adult survivors of child sexual abuse. *Journal of Traumatic Stress.* 15(3), 235-244.

Johnstone, C. (2010). *Find your power: A toolkit for resilience and positive change* (2nd ed.). Hampshire, UK: Permanent Publications.

Kassamali, T (1998). *Muslim family lessons: Raising children.* Richmond, B.C.: Tayyiba Publishers &Distributors.

Khalil, M. (2004). A Muslim perspective on human rights. *Society.* 41(2), 29-35.

Kocturk,T. (2003). Foetal development and breastfeeding in early texts of the Islamic tradition. *Acta Paediatr.* 92, 617-620.

Lamb, M.E. (1999). Child witnesses: recent research on children's accounts of forensically relevant experiences. *Applied Developmental Science.* 3(1), 2-5.

Langeland, W. & Dijkstra, S. (1995). Breaking the intergenerational transmission of child abuse: beyond the mother-child relationship. *Child Abuse Review.* 4, 4-13.

Lewin, K. (1947). Frontiers in group dynamics. In D. Cartwright (Ed.), *Field Theory in Social Science* (pp. 188-237). London, England: Social Science Paperbacks.

Lickona, T. (1996). Eleven principles of effective character education. *The Journal of Moral Education.* 25(1), 93 - 100.

MacQueen, K. (2008). Rescuing children from toxic divorce. (pp.12-13) *Maclean's* news magazine. June 16, 2008 Issue. Toronto, Ontario- Canada.

Mahdavi, S. (2008). Islam. *Encyclopedia of Children and Childhood in History and Society.* Retrieved 15 January, 2013, from http://www.faqs.org/childhood/In-Ke/Islam.html.

Mahmood, S. (2004). A word about ourselves. *Journal of Muslim Minority Affairs.* 24 (1), 5-7.

Makhoul, J., Shayboub, R., and Jamal, J. (2004). The silent determinant of child labor. *Journal of Children & Poverty.* 10 (2), 131-147.

Matsumoto, D. (2007). Culture, context, and behavior. *Journal of Personality.* 75 (6), 1285-1319.

Mckee, L., Roland, E., Coffelt, N., Olson, A.L., Forehand, R., Massari, C., Jones, D., Gaffney, C.A., Zens, M.S. (2007). Harsh discipline and child problem behaviors: The roles of positive parenting and gender. *Journal of Family Violence.* 22, 187-196.

McLeer, S.V., Deblinger, E., Atkins, M.S., Foa, E.B., and Ralphe, D. (1988). Post-traumatic stress disorder in sexually abused children. *Journal of the American Academy of Child and Adolescent Psychiatry.* 21, 650-654.

Mellody, P., Miller, A.W., & Miller, J.K. (2003). *Facing co-dependence: What it is, where it comes from, how it sabotages our lives.* San Francisco, USA: Harper.

Messman, T. L. & Long, P.J. (1996). Child sexual abuse and its relationship to revictimization in adult women: a review. *Clinical Psychological Review.* 16, 397-420.

Metcalfe, B.D. (2007). Gender and human resource management in the Middle East. *International Journal of Human Resource Management.* 18 (1), 54-74

Mijnarends, E. (1993). Shared values across cultures: A conference report. An uncertain future (Edited by Lynch, M.A.) *Child Abuse Review.* 2, 212-216.

Mtango, S. (2004). A state of oppression? Women's rights in Saudi Arabia. *Asia-Pacific Journal on Human Rights and the Law.* 1, 49-67.

Muslim Academy. (2013). *Does Islam allow parents to treat boys and girls differently?* Retrieved 1 March, 2014, from: http://muslim-academy.com/islam-allow-parents-treat-boys-girls-differently/#sthash.vsbe7QS8.dpuf

Nafisi, A. (2004). *Reading Lolita in Tehran: A memoir in books.* New York: Random House.

Okasha, A., Karam, E., Okasha, T. (2012). Mental health services in the Arab world. *World Psychiatry.* 11 (1), 52-54.

O'Sullivan, B. (2012). The alienated child. *The Irish Social Worker.* Winter (2012), 13-16.

Perry, B.D. (1997). Incubated in terror: neurodevelopmental factors in the cycle of violence. In J. Osofsky (Ed.), *Children, Youth and Violence: The Search for Solutions.* New York: Guilford Press.

Pianta, R., Egeland, B., & Erickson, M. (1989). The antecedents of maltreatment: Results of the mother-child interaction research project. In D. Cicchetti & V. Carlson (Eds.), *Child Maltreatment: Theory and Research on the Causes and Consequences of Child Abuse and Neglect* (pp. 203-253). New York: Cambridge University Press.

Polansky, N., Chalmers, M.A., Buttenwieser, E.W., & Williams, D.P. (1981). *The damaged parent: An anatomy of child neglect.* Chicago: University of Chicago Press.

Polonko, K.A. (2006). Exploring assumptions about child neglect in relation to the broader field of child maltreatment. *Journal of Health & Human Services Administration.* 29 (3), 260-284.

Price, D. (2002). Islam and human rights: A case of deceptive appearances. *Journal for the Scientific Study of Religion.* 41(2), 213-225.

Rahaei, S. (2012). The rights of refugee women and children in Islam. *Forced Migration Review.* June, 4-5.

Rassekh, S. (2001). *The challenges facing education and curriculum development at the beginning of the twenty-first century.* Retrieved 11 December 2010 from: http://www.ibe.unesco.org/curriculum/GulfStatesProjectsPdf/omanIras.pdf.

Romeo, F.F. (2000). Child abuse and report cards. *Education.* 120 (3), 438-441.

Sadowski, L.S., Hunter, W.M., Bangdiwala, S.I., and Munoz, S.R. (2004). The world studies of abuse in the family environment (WorldSAFE): a model of a multi-national study of family violence. *Injury Control and Safety Promotion.* 11(2), 81-90.

Safi, O. (2009). *Memories of Muhammad.* New York: HarperCollins.

Silvers, L. (2008). "In the book we have left out nothing": The ethical problem of the existence of Verse 4:34 in the Qur'an. *Comparative Islamic Studies.* doi: 10.558/CISv2i2.171, 171-180.

Salovey, P., & Mayer, J. (1990). Emotional intelligence. Imagination, cognition, and personality, 9(3), 185-211.

Sorabji, R. (1973-1974). Aristotle on the role of intellect in virtue. *Proceedings of the Aristotelian Society.* New Series, 74, 107-129.

Springer, K.W., Sheridan, J., Kuo, D., and Carnes, M. (2003). The long-term health outcomes of childhood abuse: an overview and a call to action. *Journal of General Internal Medicine.* 18, 864-870.

Squire, L. (1992). Memory and the hippocampus: A synthesis of findings with rats, monkeys, and humans. *Psychological Review.* 19, 195-231.

Stacey, A. (2008). *Health in Islam.* Accessed on January 19, 2014. Available on the IslamReligion.com website at: http://www.islamreligion.com/articles/1891/

Stacey, A. (2010). *What Islam Says About Children: Custody and Fairness.* Accessed on January 15, 2014. Available on the IslamReligion.com website at: http://www.islamreligion.com/articles/3662/# ftnref21341.

Strauss, M.A. (2001). *Beating the devil out of them: Corporal punishment in American families and its effects on children* (2nd ed.). New Brunswick, NJ: Transaction Publishers.

Strauss, M.A. and Paschall, M. (2009). Corporal punishment by mothers and development of children's cognitive ability: A longitudinal study of two nationally representative age cohorts. *Journal of Aggression, Maltreatment & Trauma.* 18, 1-25.

Takrouri, M.S. (2007). Editorial child abuse in medical practice. *The Internet Journal of Health.* 6(2).

Tanios, C. Y., Abou-Saleh, M.T., Karam, A.N., Salamoun, M.M., Mneimneh, Z.N., and Karam, E.G. (2009). The epidemiology of anxiety disorders in the Arab world: A review. *Journal of Anxiety Disorders.* 23, 409-419.

Tayeb, M. (1997). Islamic revival in Asia and human resource management. *Employee Relations.* 19(4), 352-64.

United Nations. (2009). *The demographic profile of the Arab countries. Beirut, Lebanon: The population and social development section of the social development division, economic and social commission for Western Asia (ESCWA).* Retrieved 15 January 2013, from: http://www.escwa.un.org/information/publications/edit/upload/sdd-09-TP9.pdf

Usta, J. and Farver, J. (2010). Child sexual abuse in Lebanon during war and peace. *Child: Care, Health and Development.* 36(3), 361-368.

Veltkamp, L.J., Miller, T.W., and Silman, M. (1994). Adult non-survivors: the failure to cope of victims of child abuse. *Child Psychiatry and Human Development.* 24(4), 231-243.

Warshak, R. (2003). *Divorce Poison: protecting the parent-child bond from a vindictive ex.* New York, USA: Harper Paperbacks.

Weinberg, K. & Tronick, E. (1998). Emotional care of the at-risk infant: Emotional characteristics of infants associated with maternal depression and anxiety. *Paediatrics.* 102 (5), 1298-1304.

World Health Organization (WHO), International Society for the Prevention of Child Abuse and Neglect (ISPCAN) (2006). *Preventing Child Maltreatment: A Guide to Taking Action and Generating Evidence.* Geneva, Switzerland.

Widom, C.S. (1989). Does violence beget violence? A critical examination of the literature. *Psychological Bulletin.* 106, 3-28.

Widom, C.S. (1999). Posttraumatic stress disorder in abused and neglected children grown up. *American Journal of Psychiatry.* 156(8),1223-1229.

Wolfe, D. A. (1985). Child-abusive parents: An empirical review and analysis. *Psychological Bulletin.* 97(3), 462-482.

World DataBank of the World Bank. (2012). Gender Statistics Highlights from 2012 World Development Report. Retrieved 28 February, 2014, from: http://databank.worldbank.org/data/home.aspx

Yahia, M. (2012). Dealing with mental illness in the Middle East. Interview with Dr. Ziad Kronfol. *Nature Middle East.* Retrieved 18 February, 2014, from: http://www.nature.com/nmiddleeast/2012/120724/full/nmiddleeast.2012.103.html

Zahraa, M. & Malek, Normi A. (1998). The concept of custody in Islamic law. *Arab Law Quarterly.* 155-177.

About The Author

Nina Abdul Razzak was born on September 23, 1969 in Beirut, Lebanon to Palestinian parents. She currently works as an Assistant Professor of Educational Psychology and Leadership and resides in the Kingdom of Bahrain. Dr. Abdul Razzak has many years of experience teaching at all school levels as well as in higher education.

As a researcher, she has written and published in a variety of areas like: best practices in education, technology access and integration in schools, teachers' professional development, the effects of child maltreatment, and gender-related issues. She is also a reviewer on a number of international scientific journals and is the founder and managing editor of her own international peer-reviewed journal, the *Journal of Teaching and Teacher Education,* which is sponsored and funded by her university, the University of Bahrain.

One of Dr. Abdul Razzak's major hobbies is writing for leisure and she is currently an author of two published literary works: a collection of poems and a memoir. Before her book *'My Rights Are Divine: A Closer Look At Children's Rights in the Muslim Arab World',* she self-published a memoir called *'A Year To Forget: A Year Spent in Agony',* which focused on a very painful year of her life while suffering with loss, illness, and a number of other unfortunate events. Prior to that, she had self-published a collection of poems focusing on her status and outlook as a second-generation Palestinian refugee. She composed and collected those poems over a number of years and finally published them in a book, called *'Displaced Treasures: A Collection of Poems of Exile'.* Her work was well-received by many readers in the Arabian Gulf region, especially by those who could relate to the Palestinian experiences of displacement, exile, and occupation.

Her limited but successful experiences at publishing have encouraged her to pursue writing even further as a dream that she has had from a very young age. To her, writing is a peaceful outlet through which she can reflect on, and clearly express, her true self and feelings. She tends to prefer writing about things she is strongly passionate about, like for example, human suffering, her original homeland Palestine, or her own personal experiences. She hopes to continue writing till her last breath, for she strongly believes that as long as one is able to think and feel, one is able to create.

Dr. Abdul Razzak welcomes inquiries at her email address: ninarazzak@yahoo.com.

www.ingramcontent.com/pod-product-compliance
Lightning Source LLC
Chambersburg PA
CBHW020529290526
45786CB00002B/806